Oracle Alchemy

THE ART OF TRANSFORMATION IN LIFE AND CARD READING

Ana Cortez
illustrations by CJ Freeman

ANA CORTEZ

Oracle Alchemy © Ana Cortez

All images © Ana Cortez

All rights reserved.

Two Sisters Press
P.O.Box 5613
Santa Fe, NM 87502

http://www.anacortez.com

Cover and interior illustrations by C.J. Freeman.

Thank you for purchasing "Oracle Alchemy." Visit www.anacortez.com/alchemybonus for outtakes and bonus material not included in the final draft of this book.

DEDICATION

This book is dedicated to my late father, C.J. Freeman, who is ultimately responsible for all this madness.

CONTENTS

	Acknowledgments	viii
	Introduction: Dispelling the Pointy Cap	ix
	PART ONE: *Fractured Fairy Tales*	
1	Once Upon A Time	Pg 3
2	Mystery in the Corn	Pg 9
3	Desperate Diseases Require Desperate Remedies, or Not at All	Pg 17
4	It Doesn't Get Any Better Than This	Pg 23
5	The Set Up	Pg 31
6	King of Hearts	Pg 33
7	Birds of a Feather	Pg 41
8	Happily Ever After	Pg 47
9	Cauldron in Green	Pg 51
	PART TWO: *Transformational Card Reading*	
	Introduction: Out From Under the Covers	Pg 57
10	Think Impossible	Pg 61
11	Your Super Power	Pg 67
12	Jumper Cables	Pg 71
13	Your Flying Machine	Pg 77
14	The Golden Ring	Pg 83
15	Puppet Strings	Pg 91
16	The Doors	Pg 99
17	The Acid Test: Ridiculous Happiness	Pg 107
18	Spider Vision	Pg 111

19	Weapons and Playthings	Pg 117
	In Closing	Pg 125
	About the Author/Illustrator	Pg 129

Table of Illustrations

"Sol," King of Clubs, from The Playing Card Oracles Divination Deck	Pg xiii
The Early Days (Ana)	Pg 4
The Fab Four	Pg 7
"The Enemies," 2 of Spades, from The Playing Card Oracles Divination Deck	Pg 10
"Carnival of Lost Souls," 9 of Spades, from The Picture Book of Fate and Fortune.	Pg 15
"Leah," Queen of Clubs, from The Picture Book of Fate and Fortune	Pg 19
"Fata Morgana," 5 of Hearts, from The Playing Card Oracles, Alchemy Edition Deck	Pg 22
"Terrene," Lady of Spades, no deck associated	Pg 26
"Sword of Healing," 7 of Hearts, from The Playing Card Oracles Divination Deck	Pg 29
What a Handful (C.J. Freeman)	Pg 32
"Nichomiah," King of Hearts, from The Playing Card Oracles, Alchemy Edition	Pg 36
"Wicca," 8 of Clubs, from The Playing Card Oracles, Alchemy Edition Deck	Pg. 39
A Portrait of Lainey	Pg 43
Turn a Card Dearie, no deck associated	Pg 45

The Laddy Card, Joker from The Picture Book of Fate and Fortune	Pg 50
"The Three Sisters," 3 of Hearts, no deck associated	Pg 54
"Leah," Queen of Clubs, from The Playing Card Oracles Divination Deck	Pg 60
"Déja," Queen of Hearts, no deck associated	Pg 65
"The Necklace," 3 of Diamonds, The Playing Card Oracles Divination Deck	Pg 70
"Passion," Ace of Hearts, The Playing Card Oracles, Alchemy Edition Deck	Pg 76
"Leah and Sol," no deck associated with this version of Leah, Sol is from The Playing Card Oracles, Alchemy Edition Deck	Pg 81
"Ethra," Ace of Clubs, from The Playing Card Oracles Divination Deck	Pg 90
"The Severed Head," 3 of Diamonds, from The Playing Card Oracles, Alchemy Edition Deck	Pg 98
"Gawain and Bluebeard," both from The Playing Card Oracles, Alchemy Edition Deck	Pg 99
From an Early Notebook, no deck associated	Pg 106
"Fortuna," Lady of Clubs, from The Playing Card Oracles Divination Deck	Pg 110
"Throne of Spiders," 9 of Spades, from The Playing Card Oracles Divination Deck	Pg 115
"The Sword," appearing as the 7 in all 4 suits, from The Playing Card Oracles, Alchemy Edition Deck	Pg 124
"Terrene," Lady of Spades, from The Picture Book of Fate and Fortune	Pg 127
Author and Illustrator Photo	Pg 129

Acknowledgments

Special thanks to my adorable husband, Todd, who keeps me looking forward to every single day; to Freeman and Nanette, who shine in my heart as inextinguishable luminaries; to Grandma, whose help has made absolutely everything possible; to my whole entire loving network of family and friends; to the wonderful fans and supporters of *The Playing Card Oracles*; and deep gratitude to Silvia Polivoy and Zoe 7.

INTRODUCTION:
DISPELLING THE POINTY CAP

THE WORD ALCHEMY, TO ME, has always had this sort of luster, this aura of great appeal shrouded beneath a near impenetrable veil of obscurity. Over the years, looking for a starting point for further exploration, I have bumped up against the same discouraging definition of alchemy over and over again: "the medieval forerunner of chemistry, mainly concerned with attempts to turn base metals into gold." What does this even mean? From this I picture some scraggly haired magician, pointy cap askew, hunched over a little blow torch and some aluminum. Really? Couldn't those old wizards think of something better to do than sit around trying to get rich off of scrap metal?

But what if this worn out, simplistic definition is a *metaphor* for some other more enticing, more relevant process? And what if it is available to you, now, as a means of transforming *yourself* - radically, chemically, and forever - from ordinary "base metal" into a being of realized super-human potential, a "gold," of sorts? And *why not?*

Secrets once hidden deep within the bowels of clandestine societies are now plastered on the covers of magazines for all to see. There is truly NOTHING that stands between you and your wildest dreams, except perhaps your own desire. And would you dare to reach for treasure far surpassing material achievement?

There is an alchemist inside of you, and it is what you were made for. I assert it is the unavoidable destination point of each and every one of us to become master of miracles, master of our own being, and yes, our own destiny. The only question remaining is *when* - when to get serious about the journey?

So this book is for the "serious" reader, and included within its' pages you will find two perspectives, two main but very differing sections that address the pursuit of an alchemical life in different ways. The first section, or "Part One," is a bit of a warm up for "Part Two." It follows the story of my own early life, a condensed memoir of events that led ultimately to my calling as an "oracle." It includes lessons which were at once practical but also foundational for other, later lessons in personal alchemy.

Part Two is a real switch from Part One. You could say it is a book on card reading, but I can guarantee it is like no other book on card reading you may have seen. It is pure, undiluted BOOTLEG. Rather than tell you what this or that card meaning is, or what formation to lay cards out in like most card reading books, it explains how to use *any* method of card reading and turn it into a sacred practice of personal communion, a practice of alchemical transformation.

You see, my problem is every time I have picked up a book on card reading I have been looking for something different. I am looking for that special something I can't quite put my finger on but always just seems to be missing. All the books seem the same to me. I think the truth is that what I have really been looking for my whole adult life could never be told to me by someone else. It had to come from me.

So this, like my first book on card reading (*The Playing Card Oracles,*) is unlike any other book or method of card reading. It has been birthed straight out of my soul, kicking and screaming.

It is what quenches my own thirst for something that feels substantial to me, so in a very real way I wrote this book for myself. It may or may not be for you. Like I say, it's pure bootleg concentrate so you need a hankering for something strong.

Another thing about this book that makes it very different is not only do the techniques given apply to any method of card reading, any kind of cards, but to any and all of *life*. Because card reading is the perfect metaphor for life. And to be a skilled practitioner is to be skilled at life. So we can be magicians in the card parlor and it schools us how to be magicians in the world. We can have the life of our dreams using card reading techniques.

So this book will encourage you to dream big and break down all kinds of personal barriers. So again, only you can know if this sort of thing interests you or not. It is not the most comfortable work. In fact, I have jumped in the boiling pot so many times in my life, it is what has allowed me to write a book like this. So I like to think what is contained in these pages can act as some serious guidance for someone like me, who is looking for their own truth.

I believe that card readers have the potential to become more than what we have been made to feel we are from a societal perspective - something along the order of cockroaches. I believe we are the new priests and priestesses of the time to come, along with other practitioners of the divinatory arts. My wish for this book is that it helps pave the way into this bright era. Oracles were once esteemed in the past, and they can be again. We have the potential. Now we need the training.

And some final words of advice before you delve headlong into this book of no return. The path of the "truth seeker," the "oracle alchemist," is a solitary path, indeed. The journey must be personal, or it has no value. And the road is not clear. It is hazy. We are way makers. And we find "glimmering nuggets" where we will, seekers of something the main stream will never quite understand.

So take what you will. And may it be of assistance to you, dear reader, in the production of something very precious within your own being: a "gold," of sorts.

KING OF ALCHEMY

THE FIRST OF A NUMBER OF FEATURED IMAGES PROVIDING ORACULAR STEPPING STONES THROUGH THE TEXT. THIS, LIKE THE OTHERS, IS AN ILLUSTRATION BY MY FATHER, C.J. FREEMAN. TOGETHER THEY ARE A SMALL REPRESENTATION OF A LARGE BODY OF ARTWORK FOR DIVINATION WITH PLAYING CARDS LEFT BEHIND WHEN HE PASSED IN 2010. NOT ONLY DO THESE TIE CONCEPTS IN THE TEXT TO ORACLE IMAGERY, TO GET YOU "THINKING IN CARDS," BUT POTENTIALLY ACT AS PORTALS INTO GREATER MYSTERIES THAN WORDS ALONE CAN COMMUNICATE. THIS IS THEIR BEAUTY.

I FEEL IT IS FITTING HERE TO HAVE THE KING OF ALCHEMY, SOL, AND HIS STUDIES OF SYMBOLS AND SECRET KNOWLEDGE. THIS IS THE ORIGINAL PEN AND INK, THE LAST KING OF CLUBS MY DAD EVER ILLUSTRATED.

"...he was seen disappearing forever through the door, but left behind a few flakes of gold - the fruit of a successful alchemical transmutation, and a mysterious paper full of enigmas and magic symbols that would contain the secret of the Philosopher's Stone."

-- from legend transmitted in 1802 by Francesco Girolamo Cancellieri

PART ONE

Fractured Fairy Tales

Once Upon a Time

CHILDHOOD WAS AN OPUS OF JUXTAPOSITIONS, setting into motion the strange orbit that I can now look back on and call my wonderful and unusual life. As the first born, I was strongly influenced by my very eccentric, metaphysically oriented father, (C.J. Freeman,) as well as by the very opposite, very practical orientations of my double Virgo mother.

The place we lived reflected stark contradictions, as well. I'll never forget the white walls and cheap carpet of our low rent, mouse infested apartment - kept tidy by my mother and surprisingly accentuated with extravagant and bizarre antiques, compliments of my father.

Enter the ancient Chinese curse, "May you have an interesting life."

Set within the heart of the still somewhat untamed midwestern United States, I learned early on, as neighborhood friends would exit our house in a wide-eyed glaze, that somehow life was going to be different for me.

THE EARLY DAYS

The Tea Party, or "What I learned from Tea"

Tea was a big thing at my house - pretend tea, that is. My room was quite the gathering place for social affairs of the invisible. There was always Pink Oink in attendance (a "regular",) as well as Pink Bunny, Baby Drowsy, and numerous others that had to take rotations (only so many chairs.) It was always a special occasion when Howard would attend. Howard was a character my dad would play: the misunderstood monster in the house.

When word came via my mother that Howard would be in attendance, an extra chair would need to be set and an extra place setting, and maybe an extra plate of invisible cookies. Then, eventually, there would be a knock at the bedroom door. Howard looked like a giant as he entered my room. He was too big for everything. He was the biggest one at the tea party by far, and always a big problem.

Howard could never do anything right, but how could you get mad at him? His classic move was eating the plastic forks, which was always upsetting. He spoke no intelligible words, only moaning noises - like Frankenstein fresh off the slab - so it was better to ask very simple yes and no questions of Howard.

It was always a mix of relief and feeling sorry for Howard when he would finally leave, head hanging low as he shuffled from the room. What I learned from these "tea parties" is: A) Be tolerant of those less fortunate, and B) Go to your kids tea parties. Go out of your way to make those you love feel loved by giving them your time. Time is worth a lot more than money.

My parents paid attention to me and showed me I was a priority. This is how I knew they loved me - not because they said they loved me or bought me stuff. I remember, for example, my mom made a "car" for me out of old appliance boxes, with room for driver and three passengers, and doors that opened and closed. I remember the kids in the neighborhood lined up in our hallway, waiting their turn to sit in my cardboard car. Mom was interested in me, and spent time asking me questions and having conversations with me.

Dad taught me how to soap the neighbors windows on Halloween, and how to a play a decent game of chess by the time I was 5 or maybe 6 years old. Always there were stories at bedtime, and many, many other fond memories of love, care, and play.

But unrest was growing in the underworld of my fantasy existence. The only thing there seemed to be money for was decadent antiques which my dad would appear with, all the while my mother was scraping for coins to buy food. And the fights escalated.

THE FAB FOUR: MOM, DAD, SIS, AND ME

Mystery in the Corn

This early chapter of my life ended at about the age of 7, when my parents decided to divorce. This was about 1971, when very few kids had divorced parents. I remember my uncle trying delicately to explain to me what the word meant.

The only way to describe what happened following this "family announcement" is that it seemed the whole world was being ripped in half. It was the cataclysmic splitting of the atom that was our little family nucleus. There was kidnapping, car accidents, affairs, court room drama, and I don't know what else. I walked out in front of a car during this time - a station wagon going about 35 mph - and am lucky I lived. Mom came inches from death in a separate freak wreck that smashed her face and tore open her internal organs. She was just sitting at a stop light when another car came flying right into her.

I remember this defining moment in the middle of it all when my mom's Mom had a hold of one of my arms and Dad the other, and they were pulling in opposite directions, like in a cartoon. I think they were really just acting out my own impossible desire. After all, how could I live without either one?

If only there had been a zipper right down my middle, I would have gladly separated myself right then and there.

AND THE WORLD IS TORN IN TWO...

DRAWING FOR THE 2 OF SPADES, WHICH EVENTUALLY BECAME A PART OF *THE PLAYING CARD ORACLES DIVINATION DECK*. CARDS OF THE NUMBER TWO SYMBOLIZE THE FIRST DIVISION, THE PRIMAL SPLIT FOLLOWING THE WHOLENESS THAT IS THE ACE. SPADES IS THE SUIT OF EARTH, SIGNIFYING CORPORAL REALITIES AND TOGETHER THE NUMBER AND THE ELEMENT DEFINE THIS CARD, WHICH IS APTLY REPRESENTED BY THESE TWO, STUBBORN OLD CODGERS.

I truly believe the one thing that got me through all the crap and the reason why I actually turned out pretty good in the end is because I always knew beyond a doubt I was loved. No matter how screwed up everything got, I knew my dad and mom each loved me with their whole entire heart, and that would never change. That was my rock - the only one I needed.

Well, the nuclear debris finally began to settle, and I found my young self passing untold amounts of time in closets. It just felt natural there. Come to think of it, it was actually safer there - a good decision on my part since I was literally moving through my days in a state of shock (hence the walking in front of a moving car.) Although dark, a closet has it's bonus features. It is restful, predictable - a womb of sorts.

Years later, going through my own divorce, I quite curiously found myself once again crawling into closets - an unexpected echo from so many years gone by. It seems there are times in life when we *must* go inward, and if we do not volunteer this, then life will thrust it upon us through circumstances beyond our control. And so I know this now, and this rhythm between "turning to face the sun" and retreating to my own underworld strengthens me, much like a breath. And I find it is a rare knowing to actually incorporate into one's life.

Well, years of adolescence passed with lots of time outside: lying in the grass looking at clouds, gymnastics in the yard, mischief at night in the neighborhood, and more or less running loose with a single mom who was working a lot and spending time with boyfriends that just weren't that interested in myself or my younger sister. Babysitters didn't really give a shit, and it was just as well for me. I preferred to entertain myself.

High school began, and the joys of alcohol and boys blossomed before me. This course of events, which seemed as normal as a Nebraska apple pie, took an abrupt turn, however, as I waltzed into the sink hole of an eating disorder. In hind sight, this proved to be one of my most valuable life experiences, for which I remain deeply grateful. It changed the course of my life forever, and prepared necessary ground for future challenges I could not as yet anticipate.

It was at this time Mom and I were becoming increasingly distant as the eating disorder, however unexplainable, seemed to embody an act of defiance. Everyone in the family was at a loss as to how to tame the beast that was growing inside of me. Beginning as anorexia, then later flipping to the opposite side of the same coin, bulimia, I became more and more anti-social and turned once again to my own confusing inner worlds.

The relocation of my bedroom downstairs at this time corresponded not only to the growing rift between myself the rest of the family, but also to the precarious decent into hidden realms of my own being. In the cool and windowless cement hollow lovingly referred to as "the basement," I began having out of body experiences, and in the infernal blackness encountered creatures neither human nor animal, voices chanting in unknown languages, and other things nobody wanted to hear about. Dad seemed the one person who might "get it," and our limited communication at that time was very precious to me. On his recommendation I began reading Carlos Castenada, which eventually became a very pivotal text for me. My friends changed from jocks to the kids who wore black, and the elusive little "issue" with food led me down a rabbit hole from which I would never quite fully return.

It is important to realize that this was the late 1970's, and eating disorders, especially out in the cornfields, were a thing of mystery. Who had even heard of such a thing? An eating disorder? What's that? Must be some kind of fancy thing people in New York get.

When I was anorexic, I wound up at the gynecologist's office, of all places. The old-timey doc gave me some thyroid medication and the words "pig out," which ring in my head to this day. Following this advice, the very strictly monitored regime of anorexia spiraled into the very out of control bulimia in no time. The weight piled on at record speed, the landscape of my white skin bursting to reveal screaming red ravines. And, after an epic failure at Weight Watchers, I was neatly deposited at the shrink's.

One visit with the lady with the ruffled collar, politely asking questions about what I liked and didn't like about my mother, and I realized just how on my own I really was. No one could understand why I couldn't just "go on a diet," and no one understood just how dangerous the monster I was facing. Shortly after this, I moved away from home and the amber fields of the Midwest and never looked back. At least I knew where a few of the answers *weren't*.

Living on my own, a new level of wretchedness set in. I lived like a servant of evil, existing to feed "the beast." Literally wearing clothes found in the dumpster, and eeking by on a part-time minimum wage from Baskin and Robbins Ice Cream, the world was fast passing me by. I was utterly alone, searching for a friend at the bottom of a sticky cardboard bucket, and observing as if from inside a glass bell how others my age went on dates and made exciting plans for the future. My future plans consisted of the tantalizing decision between Pralines and

Cream or Chocolate Chip Mint.

And at some point, I remember having the realization that eventually it would only be me or "it" left standing. I realized this damn thing could actually take my life, and I pictured myself as the cowboy in an old movie, nervously adjusting my holster under the clock tower at noon. Would it be me or my invisible enemy after the smoke had finally settled?

"CARNIVAL OF LOST SOULS"

THIS IS THE 9 OF SPADES FROM THE FIRST SELF PUBLISHED DECK OF MY DAD'S ILLUSTRATIONS, "THE PICTURE BOOK OF FATE AND FORTUNE." THE IMAGE AND THE NAME FOR THIS CARD CAME FROM A DREAM HE HAD AT THE TIME, IN WHICH HE WENT TO SEE A FORTUNE TELLER IN A CARNIVAL. THIS CARD REPRESENTS THE MANY EARTHLY SOULS WHO ARE LOST OR TRAPPED, AND COMMONLY POINTS TO ADDICTION AND/OR PSYCHIC ATTACHMENTS.

Desperate Diseases Require Desperate Remedies, or Not at All

INSTINCTIVELY I KNEW THAT THERE WAS A WAY OUT for me, and yet it would have to be all my own. Without money or faith in anything conventional, I began meditating. I didn't know what else to do. I would frequent the nearby metaphysical bookstore, checking the bulletin board and wandering through the aisles, hoping something would fall off the shelf and hit me on the head.

And something sort of did. A little publication crossed my path that changed everything. It was called, "The Only Diet There Is," by Sondra Ray. In it, the author spoke of a relationship with food I had not heard before, but that made sense right away. She spoke of unconditional love, affirmations, and a particular kind of breath work which at that time was called "Rebirthing."

Following the trail laid out by Ms. Ray, I began working every day with affirmations and sought out a "breath coach" who, in his mercy, helped me free of charge. Looking back, everything I needed fell into place quite remarkably, even though almost nobody could understand what the hell I was up to. How could

I even explain?

I think really, sheer determination can be a miraculous factor. As voracious as the disorder was for my soul, I was equally or perhaps more voracious for the cure. I began meditating day and night on breath using "Rebirthing" techniques, and fell in love most especially with breathing in the bath. By jamming a washcloth in the overflow drain, I was able to fill the tub to near capacity and would regularly spend the night there, sleeping with my nostrils just above the surface. Rousing only to warm the water from time to time, I basked for months in circular worlds of breath, adrift within my porcelain cocoon.

From the outside looking in, still things looked pretty pathetic for a while. Still I was working as a peon at the ice cream shop, wearing clothes from the dumpster, and continually struggling to make rent. And yet, from an inside perspective, subtle shifts were occurring that heralded something significant. What occurred over this critical period could fill a whole book on it's own, but some of the more stand out events included episodes of temporary paralysis, visitations from aliens, recollections of my own birth, and vivid dream encounters with the eating disorder in different diabolical guises.

And thanks to raw perseverance, unending breath work, reams of affirmations and journaling, good spiritual texts, and the brilliant and unwavering assistance of my breath coach, Nick (insert trumpets and fireworks here,) the disorder began slowly but surely to lose it's death grip.

Turns out I never did need to figure out "what I liked and didn't like about my mother." In fact, Mom, if you're reading this, you are off the hook. Thanks for loving me always, and thank you for going through all of this with me in your own way. Thank you forever for bringing me into this world and for bringing me the life lessons I know I needed. I love you.

LEARNING TO FLY! WHEW HEW!

ANOTHER CARD, LIKE THE PREVIOUS ILLUSTRATION, FROM "THE PICTURE BOOK OF FATE AND FORTUNE." THIS IS LEAH, QUEEN OF CLUBS. CLUBS IS THE SUIT ASSOCIATED WITH THE AIR ELEMENT AND ENCOMPASSES SUCH CONCEPTS AS BREATH, DREAMS, AND WHAT A PERSON THINKS AND PROJECTS MENTALLY. SO I WAS SUPER SUBMERSED IN EVERYTHING "CLUBS" DURING THE TIME PERIOD MENTIONED IN THIS CHAPTER, TESTING OUT MY WINGS IN INVISIBLE REALMS WHILE LEARNING TO MASTER THE YUCKY EATING DISORDER. I FELT SO AKIN TO THIS CARD FOR SO LONG, IT WAS GLUED TO THE COVER OF ONE OF MY MANY JOURNALS.

Dratted Condition

Nick was an eccentric older guy who was as generous with his time as with his invaluable and unconventional insight. For example, I remember the time he insisted on accompanying me on one of my binges. He wanted to schedule an appointment. "What?" I thought to myself. "That would ruin everything!"

"This guy obviously doesn't understand the concept of a binge," I thought. "After all, a binge is secretive, "dirty," and ridden with guilt. It's not something you do in front of someone! If you don't feel super guilty, super naughty, there is something basic missing!"

But Nick was insistent, and we scheduled the embarrassing outing. He picked me up in his beater car and drove me to a pizza place in the dead of a freezing, snowy, Minnesota evening. I remember thinking how totally pointless the whole thing was.

As I recall, we were the only ones in the joint. He treated me to my favorite large sized pizza, which was completely awkward, and then refused to take even a bite. I had to eat it by myself, right in front of him. The one condition Nick set was I had to take my time, a full hour in fact, and worst of all, I had to enjoy it, really tasting and savoring each bite.

I remember staring at the clock on the wall as I ate, thinking the guy behind the counter would probably love to close up and go home early. Nick rattled off his theories about life and metaphysics as I nodded politely and chewed, glancing continually sideways to see how much longer I had to make the pizza last.

After this, my homework was to schedule a binge appointment with myself once a week. I got to pick the day and time, and I had to stick to it. "Well," I thought, "I guess I can do that, since I binge every night anyway." But again, that dratted condition: I had to slow down - actually time myself, and enjoy and taste each bite.

So there I was, each Wednesday at 6 pm, giving myself permission to eat forbidden fruit. Enjoying the food was just weird, and really screwed up the whole binge premise, as mentioned. What was formerly a guilt ridden cram fest was strangely feeling like just a nice meal with myself. And I felt growingly confused and agitated, essentially in an existential crisis.

Was eating an entire gigantic pizza by myself okay or not okay? Basic assumptions about my world were crumbling. Alone in my shitty apartment, I threw plates and even a chair across the room in exasperated efforts to resolve the growing conflicts inside me. ***What I learned was something invaluable: It was the guilt that was the monster, not the food. It was the way I ate the food - without love, without permission, that fed the beast inside of me. Wow.***

ALL WAS NOT WHAT IT SEEMED

THE ROTTEN CORE OF THE EATING DISORDER, WHO DISGUISED HERSELF AS MY COMFORT.

It Doesn't Get Any Better Than This

So I learned to love myself, to give permission to myself, and when I found myself doing things I wasn't exactly proud of, to defiantly love myself anyway. I quit "beating myself up with food," as Nick put it. And I learned to be present, and it was monu-freakin-mental.

And the eating disorder continued to unravel.

In another memorable Nick moment, I remember him saying something that truly changed the course of my life, but at the time just seemed really flip and annoying. He remarked completely casually in the middle of one of my angst episodes, "It doesn't get any better than this."

"What does *that* mean?" I charged back at him.

"It means it doesn't get any better than right now." he replied.

"Of course it does. What are you saying?" I asked again. I wasn't going to let him get away with this one.

I am saying that everything you need to be happy exists right now. It doesn't get any better than this." his voice growing louder.

He looked at me expectantly, but my mouth somehow wouldn't open.

"You keep putting your happiness off for the future. But the future isn't any better or different than right now. It's the same." he said, nearly shouting. The moment is the same!" he paused.

I'm sure if I was a dog my tail would have been between my legs at this point. I had no response, and could not admit I was actually beginning to see some sort of weird logic to what he was saying.

"The present moment is all the same!" he was really at a peak in his performance. "It's all happening right now!" he shouted fervently. "It doesn't get any better than this!"

Then he slammed his fist on the table and just stared at me, bug-eyed. I'll never forget that steely blue gaze of Nick's, made small by his red and rather large, flat face - and it was something I didn't feel like debating with.

Apparently Nick's little shit fit made an impression, because I was never quite the same after this. I had what can only be called a personal revelation. And I began to catch myself habitually telling myself that happiness would be sometime in the future, where I could never ever reach it. I believed happiness was later, never *now*. And I recognized it was a game, that just like the guilt, kept me a prisoner, shut off from what was right in front of me. The beauty and satisfaction I was seeking *were already there*, already mine, spread out before me like a banquet in the present moment. All I had to do was allow myself to experience it.

They say that bulimics don't register satisfaction from food like other people - that there is actually a chemical generated by the satisfaction that is deficient in bulimics. And this is my experience. But what if this is really a larger epidemic? What if the pandemic greed, continual search for happiness, and general lack of fulfillment that is the hallmark of modern life is really a hunger? And what if the answer is right in front of us, waiting patiently like the present moment? **Happiness is satisfaction with the now, and it is a skill that has been forgotten.**

And I'll never forget this conversation with Nick. To this very day, whenever I catch myself thinking the future will somehow be better than right this damn minute, the memory of "It doesn't get any better than this," instantly transports me smack into the present moment. It puts me into a state of gratitude as well as expectation of opportunities available *right now*.

And my life is different because of it. I know where my happiness is.

Well, the eating disorder, as mentioned earlier, changed the course of my life. And even though I "missed out" on a certain sort of "golden period" between maybe 15 and 20 years of age, in the scheme of things, it was invaluable. I learned things about myself I could never ever have received in a learning institution or in a shrink's office. And I licked that monster for good. I really never wanted an ordinary life anyway. I want extraordinary, or why bother, in my opinion.

I remember fantasizing in those early years that once the eating disorder was in the past, life would surely be smooth sailing for me. Well, this has since proved to be far from the case. Really, now, I simply recognize what happened as necessary training and preparation for challenges yet to come. The words "Know thyself," are perhaps the only words of advice I have ever needed.

ME, BECOMING BAD ASS

THIS IS ONE OF THE MANY IMAGES THAT NEVER QUITE MADE IT INTO ANY COMPLETED DECK - ONE OF MANY "SIDEWALK CRACK" ILLUSTRATIONS. MY DAD ALWAYS PARTICULARLY LIKED THIS RENDERING OF "TERRENE." I THINK IT WAS HIS FANTASY DATE, PROBABLY INSPIRED BY BRIGITTE BARDOT. MY DAD BELIEVED AND HAD CORRESPONDING HISTORICAL EVIDENCE (DETAILED IN MY FIRST BOOK, "THE PLAYING CARD ORACLES") THAT THE TEN'S IN THE PLAYING DECK WERE ONCE COURT CARDS, ORIGINALLY YOUNG FEMALES, SIMILAR TO THE WAY JACKS ARE YOUNG MALES. HIS DECKS ALWAYS HAD THIS FEATURE, A BALANCE BETWEEN MALE AND FEMALE THAT IS IDEAL FOR CARTOMANCY.

3-D Beast

I am in a dream. I am dreaming.

I am sitting at a piano, on a piano bench next to my childhood friend.

She and I are watching as the keys dance, eerily playing themselves as we sit and observe.

And I am increasingly aware of an agitation, a tension within me as I sit. With some effort, I manage to keep my composure at the keyboard, sort of "muscling" the tension to keep it beneath the surface.

Then, something new: an idea. What if I was to quit resisting this agitation within me? After all, this is a lot of work! What If I was to just "let go?"

And so relaxing into the moment, the swirling unrest within me now unrestrained rises to the surface, and I observe as my body mutates into a full grown, hideous and disfigured beast. I can feel my spine all twisted, and I am gnarling, making unholy noises. This is the eating disorder in 3-D.

"Holy shit! Can't have THAT shit going on!" I think. So with all my might, I press and strain to contain and submerge "beastie" once more into my own, seething underworld.

"Jesus Christ!! I have got to do something!" I realize. "I need help!!"

Remembering still I am in a dream, I scan my mind for someone I can call on to help. "I need the BEST help possible. Who is the

BEST rebirther?" I think. "After all, I am in a dream. I can have anyone!!"

Thinking... thinking... thinking...

Then, pausing a moment, a sobering new realization. "No. This beast is inside of ME. I am the one who must face it. I am the one best qualified to deal with this."

And so, in my mind, I turn my focus from wildly scrambling thoughts to the sensation inside of my own self, addressing "the beast" directly.

Serendipitously, just before falling asleep, I had been reading a wonderful spiritual text,* and the potent ideas presented there were still pirouetting around in my mind. So with all my heart, soul, and conviction, I blast a recalled phrase like a silver bullet straight into the heart of that drooling abomination. It is something along the lines of, "Love is all there is."

And in this moment, a strange thing happens.

Everything goes pitch black - pitch, pitch black - and silent. And I wait, and it feels like everything is suspended.

Then, within the blackness descends a burning star: a solitary and beautiful living star with sparks flying. And it is coming toward me in the darkness. And I close my eyes as it enters my solar plexus.

I awake.

---

*The text was "A Course in Miracles."

TAMING THE BEAST WITH MY "SWORD OF LOVE AND HEALING!"

THIS IS THE ORIGINAL PEN AND INK USED TO CREATE THE 7 OF HEARTS IN "THE PLAYING CARD ORACLES DIVINATION DECK." I REMEMBER ONCE GIVING AN AUTHOR'S LECTURE WHERE I PLACED ONE CARD FACE DOWN ON EACH CHAIR BEFORE ANYONE ENTERED THE ROOM, SO EVERYONE WHO ATTENDED GOT A LITTLE ONE CARD READING. AN M.D. IN THE AUDIENCE, WHO HAD ACTUALLY COME TO HEAR THE AUTHOR BEFORE ME SPEAK ABOUT A BOOK ON MATH, BECAME INCREDULOUS AFTER RECEIVING THIS CARD SHOWING THE CADUCEUS SYMBOL.

The Set Up

I DO NOT BELIEVE IN ACCIDENTS ANYMORE. I do not believe in random. And I believe that souls travel together through certain lifetimes for certain important purposes. And so I am grateful for the relationships I have.

Dad, for one, led me to parts of myself that I am particularly grateful for. I love my curiosity, for example, and my attraction to things out of the ordinary. I love my propensity for dreaming and the supernatural. All this my dad and I share. I speak in the present tense here because even though Dad (C.J. Freeman) passed a few years ago, I know we are all eternal. So he lives inside me now, as he always has.

There are certain parts of Dad that were really just so out there. I like to think I don't share all of his characteristics, entertaining as they were at family gatherings. Anyone who met "Charlie" would say he was one-of-a-kind, and that is a radical understatement.

As much as I adored my father in early years, there was no way I could see coming the momentous project we would share in later years. It was the fulfillment of a dream for both of us, a pinnacle endeavor that allowed us each to share our creative talents in a way that achieved something neither one of us could have pulled off alone. And it was all about a pack of cards.

WHAT A HANDFUL

ING OF HEARTS

As mentioned, Mom and Dad had divorced, and so growing up my sister and I usually saw Dad in arranged chunks of time such as during summer breaks or holidays, as he lived out of state. My sister was always a little freaked out by my dad. Although they loved each other, his ways were a bit too eccentric for her comfort level. Seems she was intrinsically more conservative than me from the beginning.

Like there was "Mrs. Pfeiffer," who took up residence in the spare room of Dad's house, and followed him like a loyal servant wherever he moved. Mrs. Pfeiffer was an antique dress form, cloaked in a black, victorian style outfit. No head. My sister just thought this was ridiculous. And creepy. I didn't really care. Haunted things never bothered me. In fact, I was attracted to them. The most curious part to me was how Dad got such a kick out of introducing everyone who came over to "Mrs. Pfeiffer."

Then there were "the paintings." This artistic undertaking was perhaps the most telling expression of what was really going on inside my dad's oft inexpressible inner world. My first encounter with these unusual and original works of art rendered by my father I describe in my first book, *The Playing Card Oracles*. At about 14 years old, these life sized depictions of brightly colored fantasy figures (sort of a mix between goblin and medieval) left an indelible impression on me. Each was inspired by a different card in the playing deck, but hardly a replication of anything ever seen. Dad said he liked to just "let his hand move," and see what came out. The paintings were his first foray into what would become an eventual obsession with the pack of 52.

Later I discovered that my dad actually wrote original stories, in prose, for a number of the 52 images he had painted plus other stories related to card reading, card imagery, and playing card history. All this, again, in sort of an archaic, other-world, twisted medieval style. And then, true to Charlie space cadet form, he left the entire manuscript on the city bus in Denver.* After it became clear he would never find it, he rewrote the entire thing from scratch. I suppose it was a couple hundred pages or so. Maybe the fact that it was written in rhyme and meter made it a bit easier to recreate, but still, who does that?

I remember during this period my dad was always asking my sister and I to come up with different words that rhymed with certain other words. I remember sitting with him at the shopping mall, drinking an Orange Julius, and him saying, "Do you know there are only two words in the English language that cannot be rhymed? Those words are "orange" and "silver." (He thought that was fascinating.) "Try to think of a word that rhymes with orange, for example."

So we sat there slurping our Orange Juliuses, trying to come up with words that sounded like "orange," and then "silver." But after a while we all concluded that truly nothing rhymed properly. He wanted my sister and I always to prove things for ourselves.

And there was the time that we got stuck in a whopper snow storm up on the highway in the mountains of Colorado. To fill the hours, my dad offered my sister and I a silver quarter for every line we memorized in the "Jabberwocky" by Lewis Carroll. Apparently, Dad just happened to have the complete version of *Through the Looking Glass* there in the car. Again, who does that? The quarters were spent long ago, but to this day I can still recite that whole weird poem. My dad was always doing things to stimulate imagination and encourage us to think outside the box.

*Dad never had a car after he and Mom split up. Well, he had a car once, but left the keys in it and it got stolen literally within the first week he had it. Finally he got a bike but that kept getting stolen, too. Or parts would always get stolen. So finally he had his whole bike welded into one piece, even the bell. Always there was a funny story with my dad.

KING OF HEARTS FROM "THE PAINTINGS"

I ALWAYS ASSOCIATE MY DAD WITH THIS PARTICULAR CHARACTER IN THE DECK, HIS ENERGY WAS SO EXPANSIVE, BIGGER THAN LIFE IN SO MANY WAYS. I REMEMBER HIM TAKING MY SISTER AND I DOWN INTO THE BASEMENT SO LONG AGO, WHERE HE WAS FINISHING UP THESE PAINTINGS, AND SHOWING US WHERE HE HAD WRITTEN OUR NAMES IN THE SWIRLING DESIGN OF THIS KING'S CLOAK. I ADORE THIS PAINTING. EVERYTHING SEEMS SO GELATINOUS.

Crow Dance

After high school graduation, I decided it was time to blow out of Nebraska and road trip to my dad's before heading off to college later that Fall.

I remember waiting in the living room of Dad's new place for him to arrive. It was sunny in Denver, and the porch door was open. I sat at the heavy black table, glancing from time to time to the street outside.

The house was populated with the usual, far out antiques. Like who could ever forget the glass table with the life sized black man crouching beneath it?

Ghoulish and imposing portraits hung at intervals around the room - excerpts from "the paintings" my dad had completed shortly before. The lavishly adorned "Lords" and "Ladies" looked like something out of Dracula's family tree. Was there a secret family history, I wondered?

But nothing in that old Victorian Brownstone was quite as strange as the woman who was waiting there with me.

This was Dad's latest acquisition, I thought, a woman I would eventually come to know as "Lainey." We didn't exchange any words, but Lainey was dancing, if you could call it that, in a world all her own. Looking back, I think she was nervous, me showing up unexpected and all.

I'll never forget Nina Hagen's "Nunsexmonkrock" blasting otherworldly cacophony out of Dad's monolithic sound system, and Lainey, flapping her arms and strutting around as if possessed, making strange, bird like noises. I remember thinking she looked like a crow from another planet, her black hair and black eyes accentuating the whole vision.

Lainey was beautiful and exotic, with warm colored skin and cat like eyes that curled into gentle points at the edges. Maybe it was a cat and a bird trying to live in the same body that created the whole problem with Lainey in the first place.

What did I learn from this experience, I am asking myself now that I am putting all this on paper? Well, again, I learned A) Don't be judgmental of others and be open to life's experiences, but also B) It's okay to dance like nobody's watching, but maybe save it for when nobody actually is watching, or you could wind up in the looney bin.*

*Lainey actually did spend some time in a sanitarium.

THE CROW LADY OR "WICCA"

I CHOSE THIS ORACLE IMAGE HERE BECAUSE ANY TIME I SEE CROWS NOW, I AM REMINDED OF LAINEY. NOT ONLY WAS SHE CROW LIKE IN MANY WAYS, BUT SHE WAS THE ONE WHO GOT ME LOOKING AT THE SPADES IN PLAYING CARDS AS LITTLE CROW SILHOUETTES. AS THE TEXT THAT FOLLOWS WILL DETAIL, LAINEY WAS THE FIRST TO TAKE MY DAD'S IMAGES AND USE THEM TO READ CARDS. SHE WOULD TALK OFTEN ABOUT CROWS IN HER READINGS, AS IF PEOPLE COULD POSSIBLY UNDERSTAND WHAT SHE WAS CARRYING ON ABOUT. CROWS WERE THIEVES. THEY WERE SURVIVORS, AND THEY HAD KNOWING, LIKE LAINEY.

Birds of a Feather

What followed was an interesting and fun summer for me. Lainey and I became pals. She took me under her lovely crow wing, teaching me all kinds of stuff useful for life on the fringe. Dad was busy doing stuff like working as a bartender and getting his new rock band off the ground (a different story,) but Lainey had lots of time. And so did I.

At that time, I was still in the throws of the eating disorder and as it turned out, Lainey had an eating disorder, too. So there was *that*. We especially liked cream pies, her and I. And since neither one of us had any money to speak of, we learned to get our pies in rather unscrupulous ways. Or, should I say, Lainey taught me a few "crow techniques." She and I even managed to dine on pie at the famous and very swanky Brown Palace Hotel. We also threw up pie at the famous and swanky Brown Palace Hotel.

And then there were "the cards." My dad had made Lainey her own special deck, using polaroid photos of the paintings he had done, cut and pasted onto regular Bicycle Playing Cards. And utilizing her own very brassy and shameless nature along with a little creativity, Lainey had carved out a nice little profession for herself. This was about 1982, before card reading had really taken off in the U.S.

Often I would go with Lainey, observing her doings from a little distance away. She read in the now well known "Market" in Larimer Square. At that time The Market was almost the only thing there, as downtown Denver was just coming out of a really low period. We walked several miles from my dad's to get there, through blocks and blocks of abandoned buildings, needles strewn on the sidewalks. But once at The Market, everything was bustling.

Dad told me that Lainey had approached the owner and gotten a little "audition." Lainey was likable, entertaining, and got permission to sit at one of the tables outside. Today, you could never ever get a gig like this in Larimer Square, but it was the right place and time for Lainey. She charged 5 bucks for a quickie and lured in clients like a clever kitty cat snares stray guppies.

As mentioned, Lainey was magnetic, and quite a sight in her card reading getup. With her olive skin, eyeliner out to her temples, a scarf swirled around her head, and cascades of jingles as she walked, you could say she stood out among the lunch crowd. When unsuspecting business men would cast a glance in her direction, she would snag them with her eyes. Once caught, she would reel them in with her very talented pointer finger, motioning them with a "come hither" kind of movement. As I said, the lady had brass. I've never seen anything like it, before or since.

After persuading the client to actually spit in their own hands and shuffle, Lainey would begin turning cards. Once the cards were laid out she would pass her outstretched palms over the table - and rolling her r's with an impressively acrobatic tongue, recite several made-up words. The wavy motion of her hands combined with the coiling r's spun invisible threads this way and that across those crazy, pasted together playing cards. Whoever sat at Lainey's table was in an altered state in almost no time flat.

A PORTRAIT OF LAINEY

So Lainey taught me card reading, or something like that, although Dad was the one who not only painted the unique images but also innovated the equally unique methods that Lainey used. Lainey was an eager student who was able to take my dad's many theories and ideas about card reading and give them life. She would come home after a day at The Market and share highlights of what occurred at her table with my dad. Dad thrived on her stories, and would offer feedback and advice.

Up until this time, I wasn't all that interested in card reading, but no doubt, hanging out the whole summer in this environment had put me in an altered state as well. I think what really got me in the end was the amazing correspondences that Lainey took the time to point out to me in the regular playing cards.

For instance, the fact that the whole deck corresponds to a natural calendar just really blew my mind: 52 cards, 52 weeks; 4 suits, 4 Seasons; 13 cards in each suit, 13 weeks in each season; and more. How could I not have seen this, I wondered? After all, I had spent lots of time playing card games growing up. This was cool!

Also she explained to me how the 4 suits correspond to the 4 Elements of Fire, Air, Water, and Earth, and how each card in the deck had it's own special meaning. All this entwined around numerological correspondences and Dad's detailed magical images, and a very compelling little microcosmic world began taking shape in my mind.

So after a wild and bewitching summer, I left for college. Lainey begged me to stay. I think I was her only friend besides my dad. As I recall, she wanted me to run away with her. Somehow that didn't appeal to me. Not long after, I guess she did run away, without even a note. That's what really got my dad: no note.

Dad said he was sure she left to join the circus. I think Lainey would be lucky if she got a job in the circus. Women like that need structure. Anyway, at least she had a skill now that she could take and make a little money with.

TURN A CARD, DEARIE

Happily Ever After

It was about 10 years after this curious summer before cards drifted back 'round into my life in any serious sort of way. And after that, I was caught hook, line, and sinker, and have been working with cards ever since - always only playing cards. My dad and I went on to create what is now known as *The Playing Card Oracles*, which outlines the original system of card reading innovated by my dad, but completed compliments of the two of us. As Dad so aptly put it, together collaborating on the cards, he and I became like two halves of the same brain. It was really an extraordinary creative experience, a synergy that is hard to describe.

Whereas Lainey and her eventual follow up act, Laddy,* used my dad's card images and his system, neither really contributed to any further development of what my dad had originated. When I got involved, as I say about 10 years or so after my first introduction, I could see there were pieces missing. I stared and stared at the notes I had taken earlier with Lainey, and pestered my dad about certain questions I had, but there were no answers that satisfied me. It was like a scratch I couldn't itch. Something in the sly smiles of those old, wily court figures told me there was more, and eventually, I proved myself right.

It took some years of persistence, but sure enough, in drips and drabs, my dad and I squeezed out the secrets from those old scheisters in the cards. We were delighted and amazed as each little piece emerged. The cards were talking. *They* taught *us* how they wanted to be read.

Never, ever, did he or I look to anyone else's way of reading cards, but only always looked to the cards themselves, and asked what the creators of those cards were trying to communicate through those provocative, interlocking layers of symbols. It was a very intuitive process, a prolonged meditation of sorts that felt quite natural to us both, but also I feel we were chosen for this project on some level. We had a distinct awareness that a body of knowledge was coming through. Turned out the creators of the cards were speaking in a language of energy, a language of initiation. As we looked at the 52 card deck from this perspective, everything unfolded very nicely.

It took my dad's own very original way of looking at things, his heightened attunement to worlds unseen, and his discoverist attitude to birth the system into being in the first place, but what fun are treasure maps unless they're torn in two?

*Laddy LaDoux was another "acquisition" of my father's, like another bizarre antique. Only sometimes living antiques are a pain in the ass. Laddy had substantially less charm than Lainey, and too much venom for my liking. If Lainey was a combination of a cat and a bird, Laddy was decidedly a viper. Add this to the fact she was continually crashing a car, getting locked up in jail, or otherwise causing mad havoc, and you get the general idea. I could never figure out why my dad liked hanging out with her. Maybe he didn't.

I remember the last time I saw Laddy, her long, aging form draped across my dad's leather divan, prescription bottles and makeup strewn everywhere on the carpet. There was a partially dissolved yellow pill stuck to her bottom lip and it bobbed up and down as she spoke. Dad told me she died in the sanitarium somewhere in Texas.

THE LADDY CARD

THIS WAS AN EXTRA CARD, ALMOST LIKE A JOKER CARD IN THE FIRST SELF PUBLISHED DECK. MYSELF AND MY DAUGHTER APPEARED ON THE OTHER EXTRA CARD. FUNNY, BUT THE HEART IS ACTUALLY BLACK ON THIS ONE, AS MY DAD WANTED TO ILLUSTRATE HOW THE SPADE AND THE HEART SUITS, WHEN THEY COMBINE, MAKE A MAGICAL "5TH" SUIT. THE BLACK HEART SEEMS FITTING.

Cauldron in Green

This personal account of alchemy, incomplete as it is, would be seriously remiss without at least some mention of my experiences with the sacred plant medicine, ayahuasca. Ayahuasca is a thick, gritty brew made in a traditional way by South American shaman. It is bubbled and prayed over for days, sometimes weeks, while the shaman him(her)self is undergoing a strict fast. It is serious business. In many traditions, the whole tribe partakes of the drink in sacred, night time ceremony, guided by the shaman. It is part of the way these ancient people have kept their communities in peace, health, and harmony with nature for literally thousands of years.

The drink is essentially a simple combination of plants that together allow the person ingesting it to have an experience of DMT. DMT is short for dimethyltryptamine, which is a chemical naturally present in the human body, but largely destroyed by protective mechanisms that allow one to maintain their perception of reality as they know it. Without this sort of "police protection," even brushing your own teeth would become a challenge! DMT is at peak levels during both birth and death, and it is not uncommon for those who drink ayahuasca to have a birth or death-like experience of some kind. Alternate realities emerge.

I have heard the experiences engendered by this ancient elixir referred to as "hallucinations," and this really bothers me. It seems to me it is mostly those who have never partaken of it that would think in these terms. My dad was the first one who got me questioning that old worn out word "reality," and it took me a long time to come around to what he was trying to tell me. Through ayahuasca and other encounters with the supernatural, "reality" has become a very fluid, very loose term for me. Science is now confirming that what we experience as 3-D "reality" is really just a hologram composed of 99.99% empty space. So are we all hallucinating?

The truth is there are many layers and dimensions of "reality" existing right here and now, and it is only our limited ability to perceive that keeps us locked into one particular setting on the channel changer, so to speak. And this one channel on the dial we call "reality" and everything else gets tossed into the bin labeled "illusion." And isn't that convenient? If I subscribe to this, it only means I never have to question my perceptions, which is a state I am personally not interested in.

I can say for myself, my sessions within the green cauldron of ayahuasca challenged everything I have known. And although my life is full to the brim now with twisted, gnarly chapters, it is ayahuasca that has divided it quite neatly into two. Part 1 is everything before ayahuasca and Part 2, after.

I am a different person now, living a different life. Something returned to me within the wild womb of the Brazilian rain forest - a memory, formerly covered over. And over a six year period of pilgrimage between continents and a grueling number of ceremonies, a prolonged process of deep emergence took place, a sort of peeling away. And what I found is: I am the miracle I have been waiting for.

It is true we're composed of layers - thick and numerous layers. And the closer you get to the middle, the more juicy it all becomes.

You see, there is a me I believe I am. And I live my life according to certain beliefs, according to stories. This is the me I always think of when I think of myself, the me I think of when someone says, "How are you?" It is the me that suffers, that struggles, and that feels confused and sometimes small.

But this is not all that I am. In fact this is not me at all! There is another me, only I forgot. I do not know how long this other me has existed, but it is before the me I normally think of as myself. This other me does not experience the struggling and strife of the "small me," yet is ultimately compassionate. It is wise, at peace with all of existence, and it waits but for the "small me" to join with it. It is what I am under all the layers. Sometimes it is called the Higher Self.

And this is good news for us all. *Beneath all the stories and the crust and the forgetting, is something that can never ever be taken away, no matter what. And that something is you - your essence. It is who and what you have been since you were created, and nothing more. And it is everything you want it to be and more. It is miraculous.*

And it will wait forever, of course. It has no where to go. But why? Why wait? Time is kind, allowing us to work out our stories, but it is also the lie that keeps us arms length from our own knowing - our own joy. There is a time to leap. And it appears as through a window, in moments that pass fleetingly like glimmers flashing across an otherwise dull fabric. It is a glimpse of something extraordinary in perhaps an ordinary moment, and I meet that moment with all that I am. And that is enough.

3 OF HEARTS - THE SACRED TRINITY

ANOTHER ONE OF THOSE ILLUSTRATIONS THAT NEVER MADE IT INTO ANY OF THE 3 COMPLETED DECKS, ALTHOUGH IT REMAINS ONE OF MY FAVORITES. THIS CARD REPRESENTS THE IDEA OF LAYERS, AND HOW PAST, PRESENT AND FUTURE EXIST AS ONE INSIDE OF US. THE STAR IS A KEY ELEMENT, REPRESENTING A GATEWAY OF SORTS WITHIN THE TRINITY, THE GIFT THAT IS THE PRESENT MOMENT. THIS RESONATES DEEPLY WITH WHAT WAS SHOWN TO ME IN "THE GREEN CAULDRON," AND ILLUMINATES THE NATURE OF ORACLES AND PROPHECY.

PART TWO

Transformational Card Reading

Introduction:
OUT FROM UNDER THE COVERS

In the beginning, cards and card reading, Lainey and my dad, all had it's own story line - a very separate story line from the rest of my life. I had my own interests and my own spiritual beliefs, practice, and pursuits that all seemed to follow a very different tangent than all that crazy family stuff. It was like I had two lives that didn't really mesh together, and actually seemed to conflict if I gave it much thought whatsoever.

I was reading a lot of G.I. Gurdjieff material (Gurdjieff was an Eastern Mystic) and got involved in a local study group. There was a lot of talk about Evolutionary Psychology and other sort of heady spiritual stuff, along with meditation practices and other things that I felt very drawn to. Being a "card reader" just felt incongruous, rather embarrassing in front of my more "spiritually elevated" friends.

I noticed an overriding assumption in myself as well as in others that card reading was a practice based on beliefs in things you didn't necessarily understand, on superstitions, and "magic." The Gurdjieff work, in contrast, approached spirituality from a very dry, scientific point of view.

So I kept the card reading side of myself under the covers.

Now, after many years time these two separate parts of my life have meshed together quite remarkably. They compliment one another in surprising ways, and both are better for it. My own spirituality is richer and more expanded from being a reader, and my card reading is more sophisticated and more scientific, as I constantly question my practice, asking it to become more than beliefs or "faith" in something beyond my understanding.

And if you are a card reader reading this now, you can do the same. Card reading need not be a practice in blind faith. Although difficult to comprehend from a purely physical point of view, card reading, like anything else in this world, can be understood according to spiritual laws and perspectives. Once these laws or workings are recognized, you can use them to optimize what is going on.

Fear not the test of scrutiny. It will make your practice *better*.

We as card readers are in need of more scientific perspectives, just like the world is in need of more spiritual perspectives. The way I see it, all things in the world are equally spiritual - equally wondrous, miraculous, and truly supernatural. The fact that the human heart pumps blood and the lungs breath oxygen and a human being walks around and talks and thinks, is really unbelievable if you stop and think about it. And yet we see it, can observe it, and so we develop science to try to explain it. Why not science to explain a prediction made from cards laid out on a table - or prophetic dreams, or life after death experiences? All happen.

And so science just needs to catch up - and it is. There are new fields on the outer limits of traditional thinking like Quantum Science and other recent methodologies to measure and explain more etherial occurrences. These bleed into mystic ideologies and the line between science and spirituality becomes nearly non-existent, as we transcend limited thinking on both sides of what can now be recognized as an imagined fence.

What follows are some of my own practices in card reading as they have evolved as a direct result of the nagging co-existence between card reading and my other spiritual pursuits. So the text shifts here in this next part from personal story kind of stuff to card reading practice, and yet all offer lessons that can apply directly to the alchemy of everyday living. It is not meant to be a complete how-to on card reading, but offers perspectives on some of the more transformative possibilities. The techniques given are advanced, yet simple once they are explained, and can be applied to any practice of divination, any area of *life*. For me, they have paved a lovely little curving pathway to a more fulfilling existence, and I hope this part of the book will offer the same for you. The line between life and card reading blurs, and unexpected shades of rainbow possibility emerge.

Q OF CLUBS, QUEEN OF FUTURE POSSIBILITY

THIS IMAGE SHOWS A MARKED EVOLUTION OVER THE PREVIOUS QUEEN OF CLUBS DONE JUST 2 YEARS BEFORE (SEE CHAPTER "DESPERATE DISEASES.") I REMEMBER MY DAD WAS NEARING COMPLETION OF HIS LATEST PACK OF 52, WHEN SUDDENLY A NEW STYLE EMERGED ON THE DRAWING TABLE. IT WAS AS IF SOMEONE ELSE HAD TAKEN OVER THE PROJECT. THE NEW DRAWINGS WERE SLEEKER, MORE DETAILED AND SOPHISTICATED - AND WHAT TIMING! TRUE TO "CHARLIE" FORM, MY DAD STARTED OVER (!) AND RE-MADE ALL 52 IMAGES IN THE NEW STYLE. THE QUEEN FEATURED HERE IS PART OF THAT NEW FLEET OF IMAGES, A TRULY COSMIC MEMBER OF THE COURT.

Think Impossible

So I start at the beginning.

In preparing for a reading, it is always a question of presence, of meeting the here and now moment as completely as I am able. I sense my feet on the ground, for example. I may tune into my breath. I do not want to impose anything that is going on in my life into the space I am preparing. My mind is quiet. As best as I am able, I make an open field, so to speak, for something new to enter - something divine.

I prepare as for a communion, and everything that word implies. I find for myself my readings are truly only limited by my own personal ability to access something beyond myself, as well as my own personal goals or expectations for the reading. These two things create the boundaries.

Abilities are obviously a broad topic, and will be addressed throughout this text. Abilities can be improved. Goals and expectations are something that I am continually reformulating as I change and grow. I watch as my focus shifts and matures.

I am certain that as you read this book, your own concepts of what you can achieve and what you wish for in your readings will change. For myself, it is helpful to sit and formulate in words from time to time my intention for my divinatory practice. I allow this to change as I change, but I want to be clear about it. What do I want for myself, and what do I want to give in return? I look to remove any self imposed, presumed restrictions in this regard. I allow myself to envision and aspire to the farthest reaches of my imagination. I want nothing but the highest, the utmost. But it is personal. It is mine.

Concepts of what can be achieved with a table, a deck of cards, and the miraculous instrument that is the human being need to expand. What is the most outrageous and exciting thing you can currently imagine? And what is stopping you from setting this as your goal? The logical mind is a mind of limitation and bases it's projections on what it thinks it already knows. Do we really want a future like the past? We must slay the rational mind. We are living in a quantum world but behaving like cave men. Think impossible. Think beyond your wildest dreams. Think change the world.

So, this very private intention, whether very limited or very unlimited, is the starting point for everything that ensues. Whether I have taken the time to formulate it consciously or whether it operates from somewhere in my subconscious matters not. It is there and always at work, directing energy like a traffic cop. So it behooves me to dig and examine with brutal honesty my current beliefs and initiate real conversations between different parts of my own psyche.

I personally enjoy a great feeling of hurrah uncovering any kind of limiting belief. I love subjecting the blimey beasts to ruthless scrutiny, and find it fascinating to see how actually puny and pathetic they really are once I get a real look at them. This is probably a throw back to my eating disorder days, and the months spent digging around in my subconscious for beliefs that kept the dastardly affliction in place. And it is no different for the beliefs that control and limit our daily lives and our readings. Assume nothing!!!

So let me ask you this. Do you have formulated intentions for your life? How long has it been since you revisited them? And, maybe most importantly, do they cover not only material achievements, but also emotional goals - spiritual aspects? For what are material accomplishments absent the total self?

In the wonderful book by Esther and Jerry Hicks called *The Amazing Power of Deliberate Intent,* Hicks describes a terrific little technique called "Segment Intending." This is simply setting a very clear intention before entering into any defined "segment" of time that you choose. For example, when I arrive home after a day out and about, while still sitting in the car, I formulate my desired intention for my evening at home. In the given instance I might say something to myself like, "I desire a deeply satisfying and joyful evening with my husband that leaves us both feeling closer and more in love than ever before." I close my eyes and let the words seep in. Then I get out of the car, walk into the house, and watch what happens.

This is an extremely powerful exercise that not only impacts your life in wonderful ways, but because you are working with distinct and short chunks of time you can see and measure with ease how powerful intention actually is. Intention is amazing.

And you can do the same for your readings. Set a verbal intention for any particular session with the cards, then see what happens.

And again, for myself, I do not want limitations. I want what I want, and it is only my inability to imagine that limits me. And I know this, so I let myself go wild. I push my imagination and my goals. I think quantum. I envision that every sentient being in the universe will benefit in some way from my reading. I am here to heal the whole damn ball of wax. Why not?

In comparison with this, physical preparations for a reading seem sort of mundane, which in fact, they are. Beware of getting overly focused on "physical trappings." There is nothing really required. Props are not required. The magic is in the human being. Period.

And this does not mean I do not use flowers, candles, crystals, whatever, etc..., in my readings. This is like saying I should not decorate my house because decorations are props. If it makes me happy, it is good. If it serves to remind me of my intention, even better. I do what I want. I do not set rules for myself. I set intentions. and then the actions follow.

Cards themselves are a prop of course also, and I like them. I have developed a language using them. Are they absolutely necessary? No. And so what? It is my choice and they fit with my intentions for the reading. So be it.

Regarding your choice of cards or system of divination, this is not perhaps the most critical factor in a transformational practice, although a more sophisticated system allows more room for growth. The truly critical thing is to know your system well. Be the expert. But beware of allowing your memorized knowledge to become the entirety of your reading, unless, of course, you are aspiring to be a robot.

In the beginning of this chapter I describe a reading as a time set aside for communion. To commune implies an active and lucid interchange which opens the way for new information. So I can not be on automatic.

UNFINISHED QUEEN OF HEARTS

I LOVE THE STRENGTH OF THIS QUEEN. MY DAD ALWAYS FELT THE QUEEN OF HEARTS HAD TO BE STRONG TO STAND UP TO THE QUEEN OF SPADES, AND YET HEARTS IS A DIFFERENT KIND OF STRENGTH THAN SPADES. THERE ARE SO MANY, SO VERY DIFFERENT RENDERINGS OF THE QUEEN OF HEARTS IN THE ARCHIVES, IT IS HARD TO CHOOSE MY FAVORITE. THERE IS A STILLNESS COUPLED WITH A CLARITY HERE THAT INDICATES GREAT POWER. JUST AS THIS FALCON IS TRAINED TO DO THE QUEEN'S BIDDING, OUR OWN INTENTIONS FLY FORTH INTO FUTURE REALITIES, CREATING WHAT IS YET TO BE. SO BEST TO HAVE A WELL TRAINED BIRDIE!

Your Super Power

NOW APPROACHES THE TIME IN THE READING for the formulation of a question, which flows quite naturally from the preparations for the reading discussed in the previous chapter. Know that every word of your question will invoke something from the cards. It is time to get specific. Words have vibration, history, and intention. Choose each word of the question as individual ingredients in a magical potion.

When you witness first hand how the words of a question work to invoke specific responses in the layout, you begin to understand just how powerful words are. And of course, no need to reserve this knowing for your time at the table with your cards. The more conscious your choice of words in general, the more conscious creator of your day-to-day reality you become.

This whole idea of words I find so utterly fascinating. Of course, I myself adore the art of gab, but check this out: When you have a thought about something, it exists at a certain level within your mind, but when you *speak* that thought, *you imbue it with breath*. Breath gives life to thought in a highly alchemical act.

We are creator beings, and words are what we are given to express our true nature as such. The question is, *what will you create with your super power???*

Here I cannot help but recall some very interesting little tidbits littered about in the Bible. For example, there is a very well known quotation, "In the beginning was the Word." and elsewhere, "Death and life are in the power of the tongue." Do these alone not sufficiently communicate the almighty power of what we are talking about?

When you speak, flocks of words are born from the fantastical orifice that is your mouth. On wings of breath, thoughts literally fly forth like mythological minions to gather and return to you what you have sent out. This is something out of a really weird fairy tale, and yet truth is often stranger than fiction.

So even in day-to-day life, I am always "checking in" with my words. I know what I am forming with my lips are potent incantations, beckoning future reality. When someone says, for example, "I am so sick of my job," what is being created? Of course, it is a way of speaking, a metaphor, and yet the words have life. Words are instructions for the subconscious. Imagine the same essential thought expressed as, "I am really ready for a vacation," or "I am really ready for a new job." The sentiment is the same, but what will be gathered by the minions is entirely different.

A good general guideline is use positive ways of expression versus negative. For example, "Don't hurt yourself," is better stated as, "Be careful." Each word vibrates, and the word "don't" does not cancel out the vibrations of the words that are strung along with it. Use words you want to see expanded in your life.

So in divination I get to practice this magical, alchemical art and see how my words are reflected quite instantly in the card layout. I examine my proposed inquiry word for word, and interpret the question *literally* to determine if it expresses exactly what I want to have a real conversation about. And then, as my reading progresses, I check in, and always relate the interpretation of the cards to the words of my original inquiry - exactly the way it was stated.

So formulate your question well. Ask questions that matter, and simply yet precisely articulate them. Pretend like you are no more than 5 years old when listening to your formulation.

Once you have your lovely shining question or invocation, state it out loud, animating each word consciously with breath and intention.

3 OF DIAMONDS

FROM "THE PLAYING CARD ORACLES" DECK. THIS CARD ILLUSTRATES A WOMAN TAKING SHAPE OUT OF SMOKE, AND TYPICALLY I READ THIS CARD AS THE POWER AND POSSIBILITY OF MANIFESTATION. DIAMONDS ARE THE SUIT OF LIGHT, AND HERE THESE LITTLE GEMS FORM A PATHWAY CONNECTING HIGH TO LOW. THIS GOES ALONG WITH WHAT WE ARE TALKING ABOUT IN ALL THESE BEGINNING CHAPTERS OF "PART TWO," BUT CHECK OUT SPECIFICALLY THE FIRST PAGE OF THE NEXT CHAPTER, "JUMPER CABLES."

Jumper Cables

So, after formulating the question, we come to the all important shuffle. These few fleeting moments of mixing and stirring have ultimate impact in card reading. Wake up! What results will be the blue print for everything that follows.

So for myself, I go inward, and focus on my breath. My attention is electric, and I know this. I use it to amplify the breath's innate creative power. In my own mind, *I put the breath into my cards as I shuffle them,* knowing it will literally imbue them with life.

This is like hooking up the jumper cables to Frankenstein. I am giving life to an otherwise inanimate object. I am a full fledged alchemist (insert lightning and maniacal laughter here,) activating a highly advanced scientific process combining the powers of breath and intention with the power of randomization (which we will talk about in a moment.) This is the legendary power of three at it's finest, and *I mimic the original act of creation* each time I breathe, focus intention, and churn my little stack of pasteboard cut outs.

But let us back up a moment and look more closely at what is happening within the shuffle itself, and see what we can learn from it for our burgeoning alchemical life. First let us explore a bit the whole idea of randomizing or chance.

We know that in divination, any type of divination, the starting point is something that seems random: the patterns of stones tossed on the ground, a flock of birds appearing overhead, the lines on the hand, etc... In divination, we start with something which defies our conscious control and view it from a new perspective. We adopt a new set of eyes, looking for and acknowledging intelligence in the randomness, ultimately receiving messages that are far from random.

Over history, just about anything and everything has been employed for divination. You name it: birds, turds, rocks, potatoes, tea, clouds, feathers, wind - just keep throwing out nouns and be assured at some point someone somewhere has found guidance there. This fact alone points to the exciting expansive idea that *intelligence exists omnipresent*. No matter where you are, you can be assured there is no gap whatsoever in cosmic smartness.

The fact that someone does not comprehend the meaning or intelligence within a given occurrence does not mean it isn't there. This lack of "seeing" says everything about the person observing and nothing about the thing being observed. With proper training, a person can decipher and derive meaning from anything that the untrained individual would consider "random." So this in itself makes whatever it is *not* random.

I looked up the word "random" in the dictionary and found it very telling. It says "a happening." Wow. Could anything be more vague? Seems as a society we have very little understanding of what randomness or chance actually is. But in my view, it is precisely this that is so revealing.

Could our lack of understanding simply imply that things that appear "random" originate according to laws we are as yet unable to observe? If intelligence is "omnipresent" then if we don't understand something, maybe we are looking through the wrong pair of viewing glasses.

Now I read further, "something chosen without method or conscious decision." Hmmm… Okay. If random implies something chosen without conscious decision, then wouldn't a different way of saying the same thing be something chosen with *unconscious* decision? And isn't divination all about exploring the unconscious in order to make it conscious?

I maintain that randomization or shuffling is the very act which allows our unconscious to speak. There is a reason why the age-old, tried and true practice of divination begins with a randomizing act. It is the all important acquiescence to subliminal forces that in turn initiates the conversation between light and dark.

And "the shuffle" is exactly what takes place in day-to-day life as things "happen" in which we have very little control. No matter how well we plan, life will always be a nut mix in this way. Things that we plan or can control are masterfully intertwined with things we have no way of controlling or planning for. It is and always will be a luminous dance between light and shadow, conscious and subconscious.

And we know this on some level and yet it is amazing to me the extent that we as human beings try to avoid what is unknown. It is so very primal - the caveman instinct to huddle around the fire and shun the darkness. And we wrap the unknown in all kinds of fear, spending tremendous amounts of time and mental energy in our attempts to circumvent it. And so what are we afraid of? The subconscious? Yes. Deathly afraid.

So, in the very exceptional pursuit of becoming a self realized human being we must ask ourselves the pivotal question. Is the main motivating factor of our existence about keeping the subconscious suppressed, or is the goal the transformation of misconceptions, fears, and the otherwise unsavory delicacies lurking in our very own underworld for the sake of ultimate liberation? And isn't this the same pursuit as in any method of self-knowledge, including a card reading?

Because my personal goal is to super juice the subconscious when performing the shuffle, I get my conscious mind as far out of the way as possible. My breath and the here and now moment take the forefront of my attention, and the cards "mix themselves." I know I am shuffling, but it is background as my mind observes with vague disinterest that my hands are moving the cards. I stop when I feel finished or sometimes after the completion of some kind of predetermined, self assigned counting exercise.

I am here, present, and yet out of the way. This allows me to be the greatest conduit.

It is exciting to think that people can have inside information about what is going on within their own subconscious there, in the safe environment that is the reading table, and resolve or come to terms with this information *without having to go through the actual experience of it in their own lives.*

But what does this mean?

Of course, some things which are viewed in a reading we are pleased with and want to welcome into our lives. But other things are not, and a reading can be viewed as a golden opportunity to clear out karma and short cut to a better life. We need not be afraid of readings that show things we don't like. Instead, we should be like, "Yay!" Seeing is prerequisite to shift.

When a reading touches on a fear or place of sorrow, it is a moment for bravery, a moment for listening and allowing whatever the client is ready to share come forth into the sanctuary you have prepared.

This is when the priest or priestess within you is called upon most strongly. Do not pass it by. You can apply energy work, the use of crystals, laying of hands over the cards or the person, Ho'oponopono, affirmations, whatever suits you. You have entered the inner sanctum, and your mere presence there is shifting energy. But *be there*.

True vision is devoid of partiality, and in developing the oracle within we are led into all manner of realms, in which we must learn to be present and to navigate.

So from the perspectives laid forth in this chapter, from a self-knowledge point of view, a reading is *not* about predicting the future, but *transforming* the here and now to *create* the best future possible.

ACE OF HEARTS

A CAPTIVATING CREATURE OF MY DAD'S IMAGINATION, WITH ONE EYE CLOSED AND ONE EYE OPEN. SUCH IS THE NATURE OF WHAT SWIMS BENEATH THE SURFACE OF THE HUMAN BEING: THE CONSCIOUS AND THE UNCONSCIOUS LIVING SIDE BY SIDE. INTERESTING HERE THE INCLUSION OF THE BIRD WITHIN THE HEART SUIT, THE SUIT OF WATER, WHEN CLEARLY THE BIRD IS A CREATURE OF AIR (SIMILAR TO THE QUEEN OF HEARTS DISPLAYED TWO CHAPTERS PREVIOUS.) THIS COMBINATION OF WATER AND AIR, OR EMOTION AND MIND, IS VERY MAGICAL, VERY POWERFUL, AND VERY UNUSUAL INDEED.

Your Flying Machine

The particular layout you choose, the number of cards, etc… is all personal preference. This makes not the transformation. Choose and use what you like. But know it well. Again, be the expert.

But no matter what kind of cards or layout you choose, acknowledge your cards as a book by always turning them off the deck from side to side, never "flipping" head over tail, as is commonly done in games.

As a card reader, you are in a story teller tradition. And your deck is your book of stories, only the pages are unbound so the stories are free to change. You have a little book of limited pages with infinite story telling potential.

Life is stories and people love to hear their own story, a story about them. So I create images when I speak. Memorized meanings are forgettable for the client because it is essentially a one dimensional, mental exercise. But well crafted images impact the person on multiple levels. I create a mood, an emotion, and a vessel with my words into which the rest of my reading can expand.

I am not talking about the images already depicted on your cards, although these of course are useful. I am talking about unique visions gleaned from the one-of-a-kind encounter you have each time you sit with a client. As a reader aspiring to be master of your craft, you must be ready to jump up off the page of the card and test your wings. If you want to fly, you have got to break out of your memorized meanings and the linear mind. Imagination is your flying machine.

Now we enter precarious realms indeed. For with wings of imagination strapped to your back comes the possibility of heights previously unattainable, hand-in-hand with lows previously unattainable. Imagination is a super power, just as like the words we've already talked about. And just as words have the power to heal or destroy, imagination embodies the same potentials.

How can imagination destroy, you ask? Have you not seen readings destroyed by irresponsible use of imagination? And how about people who, dabbling without skill with this aspect of their mind, plummet from intoxicating heights to the craggy cliffs of lunacy below?

I have seen it time and time again.

But to not use these wings is really a shame. Imagination is my necessary ally in readings and indispensable in the realms of the subconscious and dreams, which is the natural domain of oracles. So eventually, if I am to become master of this craft, I must pick up and use this super power. But I have to make it work for me. I do not want to be a crazy person.

My goal is supreme sanity, right alongside the ability to lucidly enter places my every day, logical mind just cannot conceive. This is the real skill.

What I find in most readers or people, for that matter, who use imagination like Russian Roulette, is that they are lacking something super basic. And that thing is what I think of as anchors, or in every day terms, reality checks.

When I am lifting off like a veritable helium balloon in my readings, I want to always establish some kind of tether to good old terra firma. This will be my life line, much like the silver cord that connects the astral to the physical when having an out-of-body experience. This is what keeps my explorations related and relevant to the here and now.

And what is this anchor exactly? It can be many different things, but it will be something that secures me to the physical. Breath, for instance, is one such potential anchor, but I have to consciously include it. The optimum reading is going to have several anchors wound together. Anchors are awesome.

Other anchors, or "reality checks" will come from my cards themselves, but let me explain it this way: Once I had a doctor of Chinese Medicine as a card reading student, and he explained to me that the art of card reading is much like the ancient art of Asian healing. In Chinese Medicine for example, there are certain indicators. The practitioner checks some basic things like the "pulses", the skin tone, the tongue, and many other things. What he/she is looking for is things which *concur*. The practitioner looks for at least two, but better three, indicators that point the same direction before giving diagnosis.

And this is exactly what happens in a good reading. One message or indicator does not constitute a solid conclusion, nor a trustworthy tether for the imagination. Look for multiple messages, conveyed in different ways, that point the same direction. A true message ripples or rings out, repeating like a rhyme throughout one and the same spread of cards. Look for this. It is your "diagnosis."

Once I have a solid interpretation of my reading in this way, using a bit of a scientific approach, I can start to play. I let my imagination fly. As long as I check in and "anchor" my forays into what I am certain about with my logical mind, the sky is the limit. I use metaphors, visions, whatever - as long as I "check in."

What I have now is this: The rational, left side of the brain, is exchanging signals and working in partnership with the fantastical right side of the brain, creating a kind of "super mind." It is what the cutting edge mind technology called "Hemi-Sync" (or *Brain Wave Synchronization*) simulates, only I am doing it all on my own, without machines and wires. Science knows that the two sides of the brain working in tandem achieve exponentially more than either half trying to limp along on it's own.

Practicing this skill in readings develops this ability which is the same used in lucid dreaming (which Robert Monroe, creator of "Hemi-Sync," was a pioneer in,) and other states of advanced consciousness. It is developing the whole of your mind to work in a way that super charges itself as signals fly back and forth between left and right. As you use this technique, you will literally grow smarter, awakening the brain, and your life and your readings will become more creative, fulfilling, and of course, super powered.

QUEEN AND KING OF CLUBS

THIS SHOWS THE ORIGINAL PAINTINGS MOUNTED ONTO REGULAR PLAYING CARDS, EXACTLY AS LAINEY USED THEM FOR HER READINGS DECADES AGO (SEE CHAPTER "BIRDS OF A FEATHER.") CLUBS IS ASSOCIATED WITH THE ELEMENT OF AIR, AND THE COMPONENT OF MIND WITHIN THE LANDSCAPE OF THE HUMAN PSYCHE. WHEREAS THE QUEEN REPRESENTS THE VISIONARY, INTUITIVE, AND CREATIVE ASPECTS, THE KING REPRESENTS THE LOGIC, BOOK LEARNING, AND PRACTICAL APPLICATION OF THE MENTAL SELF. THEY REPRESENT QUITE LITERALLY THE RIGHT AND LEFT SIDES OF THE BRAIN. SO, WHEN THE TWO COME TOGETHER IT IS A POWERFUL COMBINATION, SIGNALING THE ABILITY TO ACCESS THE WHOLE MIND, THE SKILL WHICH IS SO VERY VALUABLE IN READINGS AND IN LIFE.

The Golden Ring

BEING STUCK IN A READING HAPPENS. I used to believe that as I got better at readings, these moments would happily go away. Now, after 30 years in this profession, what I have found is this is just not the case. In actuality, what I have discovered is that it is precisely these awkward intervals of not knowing that are my shining opportunity to take the reading to a whole new level.

The technique I am about to share with you is one of the most powerful in this book, and can be applied, of course, to daily life as well as to any of your divination practices. It is an esoteric secret so profound it's importance cannot be overstated or over explored.

As a general observation, I notice readers talk a lot and typically too much. When you are under pressure to perform or be the expert, you don't want to be perceived as being at a loss, right? I find people in general are uncomfortable with silence. Why? What are we avoiding? And is it possible that what we are avoiding is the very thing we are searching for?

I am here to let you in on a little secret: The moment of "not knowing" in a reading is nothing less than the majestic approach of what can be called the void. The void is perhaps the most sacred, most misunderstood place of power in all the universe. And it is not some mystic thing "out there." It is for you right now. It is the place where the extraordinary enters your reading and your life.

In understanding the concept I am presenting here, it is helpful to consider the world of numbers. Numbers provide a language not only for math, but a profound foundation for divination and universal principle. In the instance at hand, let us relate specifically to the number zero - perhaps the most misunderstood number of all.

The zero is supposedly "nothing," and yet we know it plays a vital role in whatever equation it is in. The number ten, for example, is comprised of the number one followed by the number zero. The zero, even though it is "nothing," changes the number one completely. It allows it to ascend to a new level - to "jump" a whole nine numbers. The number zero provides the stepping stone from one order, or level, of numbers to the next.

Picture now the visual representation of the zero: a circle around open space. Again, is the open space "nothing?" Is there even such thing as "nothing?" If ever something was truly nothing, it would be a vacuum and a vacuum is something.

If what is illustrated inside the zero is truly nothing, and if nothing is ultimately a vacuum that by definition pulls in atmosphere or even objects around it, then we can now conceive of the zero as a passage way, a worm hole of sorts - an entrance or exit point.

The mythical secret of the elusive number zero is that the zero is a picture of a miraculous and wondrous abyss, held and maintained by a tenuous, circular rim. People often draw a circle, or a ring as a mystical object. But I assert it is the invisible space within the ring that is the treasure.

But what has this to do with card reading, or life, or anything? Because the abyss, the vacuum, the void, the womb, the zero, whatever you want to call it, is what we will make use of in our practice. It is the birth place of the miraculous, and when consciously applied, takes your reading from one to ten, just as the number zero takes the number one and transforms it into the number ten.

So the question is, what in our own lives and our readings can act as this miraculous magnetic nothing? Let us look to where the seeming "nothing" is, and what it is that encircles or maintains it. What if, for starters, we look to silence? Silence is the very thing that seems like "nothing" until it is explored. And more than explore, we will now become masters of silence, using it in a true act of alchemy.

Remember, in ordinary life we are accustomed to bulldozing silence. Now, I will turn my thinking around. Life is filled with spaces, little gaps. Now I will become more interested in these, and consider more carefully my use of them. With practice, I will learn to literally HOLD THEM OPEN, facilitating the birthing process, if you will.

Know first of all that holding silence is intrinsically uncomfortable. For the uninitiated, this discomfort is something to avoid. For those with inside information, however, this is precisely where the opportunity is. I am looking for the places that make me squirm.

Once alert to my possibility, the magic trick is to *defy the pull of the silence*, becoming as still as possible on all levels. This is real magic at it's finest. I am making a golden ring - the all important "rim of resistance" that surrounds this portal of mystery. And as I consciously hold this space, I build personal force - an energetic muscle. Over time, I literally become magnetic, and my life and my readings become filled with possibility, and I recognize opportunities *everywhere*.

So from a certain perspective, my job is simple. I do not need to do anything outside of resist filling open space, best as I am able. But I must always bear in mind that what I am attempting is very opposite my usual ways. It is not the knee jerk reaction.

In the sorcerer's tradition related in the Carlos Castenada books, for example, this type of effort is referred to as "not-doing," and the concept had me in loops for a long time. We are so accustomed in life to trying to figure out what to *do* all the time, but what to *not do*? And this is exactly what we are talking about here. It is the same as looking at a piece of art from the point of view of negative space. I begin to view my life this way, slithering into emptiness with all that I am, and it takes a radical chiropractic adjustment in the brain.

And as I "slither into emptiness," I notice that what I am "not-doing" is hardly noticeable to those around me. Everything appears stupendously normal. But even a fleeting moment of stillness succinctly placed can move a mountain. I am a secret agent working in invisible realms.

And never do I worry about or try to control what comes through. Seriously, it is none of my business! Exactly the same as in the birth of a child, I recognize what comes as a perfect gift, special delivery from the grand intelligence of the universe. I trust the natural process, and I know that sometimes the results or shifts that occur *are not going to be visible to me*. I am working in the void, remember? And in the void, I may literally be effecting something somewhere else in time or space. Chew on that one!

So now, in a reading, when that inevitable moment of not knowing what to say or where to go makes it's appearance, I get excited. "The void" is forming in the ethers. I must be super brave, super awake, and use what I know to receive the gift. But are you with me here? Make sure you fully understand that the void is the only possible way something outside of my current understanding can come. There is no way around it. There must be a doorway. If I do not facilitate an opening, nothing new can enter my experience - ever. I will stay in linear time/space and stop growing in my practice and in my life.

And this is the disappointing norm. The norm is filling the void with what is familiar. So I must ask myself, what is my goal? Am I willing to take a risk, or do I want safe? Do I want a future determined by the past, or do I want to be a conduit for miraculous transformation? And perhaps most importantly, how willing am I to let go of control?

And let us leave no room for ambiguousness here. True silence means not only am I not talking on the outside, but most importantly, I am not talking on the inside. Inside my mind is where the birth is taking place. So I must very honestly assess myself. Is it possible for me to stop the internal dialogue?

So I practice, and practice and practice. I breathe. I listen. I become present, and observe how the incessant flow of my thoughts is momentarily suspended. I drop a stone into the stream.

And through this wondrous abyss of silence lies everything. Why else do you think we are so petrified of it? We feel the enormity of the formlessness - the hungry inevitable. It is the whispering of the entire universe from inside of us. But be not afraid! What we are interpreting as fear is really flying in disguise.

We have all heard that each one of us is a microcosmic representation of the macrocosmic universe, but do we have an actual *experience* of this for ourselves? Do we even believe it? And is it possible that the void that births insight and premonition into our readings is akin to what science is now confirming exists in the larger universe: cosmic worm holes that facilitate travel between different dimensions of time and space? Think about it. Could this be *why* we receive insight - because we actually have an experience, if even fleeting, of something somewhere else in time or space? This is truly tantalizing, my friends.

We exit and enter this life through tunnels. We traverse dimensions, consciously or unconsciously. But if we remain unconscious then this amazing feature of our being gets used only very minimally. But what would happen to our lives if we actually knew how to *activate* this part of ourselves, for help with anything?

So it is too late for you. You cannot be as you were before reading this. Blind ignorance is not an option for you, and you will be tormented by what you know if you choose to turn the other cheek. Now you must set out to either verify or prove me wrong.

Believe it or not, I have a personal interest in you manifesting a life beyond your wildest dreams. Why? Because miracles cannot be contained. Because each time you transcend linear time and space, even for a moment, everyone you know and everyone you don't know gets the benefit. When you shift, because you *are* part of time and space, everything shifts. No effort is wasted. The planet literally re-adjusts just that much and the ripples go out beyond what can be seen and fathomed and the entire universe lets out a little gasp.

THE ACE OF CLUBS

OF ALL THE CARDS IN THE 52 CARD PACK, THIS IS THE ONE I WOULD EQUATE WITH "THE VOID." ACES ARE DOORWAYS. THEY ARE ENTRANCE POINTS. THE CLUB ACE IS DARK, MYSTERIOUS, THOUGH ETHERIAL, UNLIKE THE SPADE ACE WHICH IS HEAVY WITH EARTH. IT DRAWS US IN THOUGH WE KNOW NOT TO WHERE. MY FATHER PREFERRED THIS ACE AS HIS "SIGNATURE CARD," INSTEAD OF THE MORE TRADITIONAL ACE OF SPADES, BELIEVING IT TO BE THE MOST POWERFUL CARD IN THE PACK. THE TEXT BELOW THIS PARTICULAR RENDERING, "*THE PICTURE BOOK OF MADAME ZO*," WAS THE WORKING TITLE FOR "THE PLAYING CARD ORACLES DIVINATION DECK."

Puppet Strings

People have a tendency to resist or avoid situations they don't like. As human beings, we are professional at all kinds of ways of approaching life that actually perpetuate the very things we want to change.

But change is a funny thing. Often it seems the more I want something other than what I have, the more it eludes me. It's like the old saying, what you resist, persists. And so I find, as time passes in this profession of being card guru, I do a lot less trying to fix what I find, and a lot more looking for what needs to be embraced. But let's back up.

Always I feel my first job as a reader is to recognize that every single person on the planet has a very different life path than every single other person. So I never want to try to mash anybody into any well worn nook. I want to see each client as the completely one-of-a-kind being that they are, with a life path probably no one else can even completely understand. And that means my cards are going to have to communicate to me something I have never seen before in any other reading. So I am a life long learner, even though I have been using the same darn deck for 30 years. My brain stays young.

Mostly what I find is people are trying to live their lives according to some imagined standard, which typically causes what's called "the problem" in the first place. They think the ideal relationship should be like something out of a romantic movie, for example, or their job or money situation should conform to some sort of generic, cookie-cutter mind set. And be careful you do not fall into this trap as the reader!

So, I am looking for the thing that makes that person weird, and acknowledging the beauty in *that*. I find that just giving a person permission to be and express exactly who they are is the hugest relief in the world and one of the best things I can give a person. To be seen, acknowledged, and not judged is right about the moment in the reading when people burst into tears. A tear is a very good sign.

And this kind of release is healing in the true sense. It is why I say a good card reading is a healing. All healing is ultimately healing not of the soul, because the soul does not require healing, but of the psyche. And once the psyche heals, the other levels of our being, including physical, can heal as well. They follow naturally.

Remember energy, which is all your layout represents, is never, ever intrinsically good or bad. Always it just is. It is the resistance to what is trying to flow through that causes the pain or dysfunction. I am reminded of nature, and how its' beauty comes from the fact that it is just being itself, in all its' unexpectedness, nakedness, treachery, and bounty. And I trust that nature knows what it's doing.

I think of people as individual trees, and how beautiful each is precisely because it is completely unlike any other. So we are each a non-duplicatable expression of the infinite, providing an energetic service for the planet that no one else can fill, just by being. And in the ultimate irony, once we find peace and acceptance with what we are and what we have, it greases the wheels for change. Because in that moment, we are free.

But let's go a little deeper into this scenario of peace and acceptance. What if a person does not *like* what they have and are given, and in fact wants something different? What then?

I recently had a client, for example, who wanted to manifest her life partner, her committed relationship. She was up on the latest new age material about how to manifest her desires, and she was focusing and focusing, putting out her intention, but it had been several years and nothing was working. She was attractive, had lots of guys wanting to date her, but few she was interested in. The guys she felt attracted to came and went, as through a revolving door. Nobody would commit, and her reading showed exactly this. She was at the breaking point and could focus on little else.

So, remembering always that the reading is a depiction of the client's energy, something started to emerge. The cards clearly showed the men keeping always the back door open for quick escape, but it was *her* energy, right? How could it be otherwise? It was *her* reading, her blueprint. It was what she was emanating and the guys simply came and filled the bill. Do you see what I am saying?

Once viewing the reading from this perspective, I looked straight at her and said, "YOU are the one who doesn't want to commit." A measurable pause ensued, our eyes in a locked embrace - and then the flood gates flew open.

A stream of justifications began flowing from her mouth,

detailing how when she had committed in the past everything had turned out badly, and had been difficult to get out of. Not only that, but commitment had always stifled her own "wild goddess" self that she had come to love and cherish, and she was afraid that if she did commit and changed her mind later it would hurt people. There was all kinds of trepidation, but in her conscious mind she was convinced she wanted that dream monogamous scenario.

So be clear. The reading can always only reflect the client's energy. The layout comes to life on the table like a page in a little pop up story book, but the projector that generates the story is the client. It is the way the pure light of spirit filters through the person sitting next to you. In this instance, the woman herself was the puppet master in her own repeating scenario of rejection, projecting her secret fears onto the men in her life, so it all looked like it was happening *to* her, instead of *by* her.

And the news is: we ALL do this. Daily. We all believe that others outside of ourselves create problems by acting against our own will, but if something is happening to us, I tell you verily it has to fit or resonate with something somewhere within our own energy field. I know this is hard to hear, and I realize that this aspect of transformational card reading undoubtedly opens up a loaded topic for many. Here I will clarify with a few sentences and for those who are interested, further follow up is added in a footnote.*

Regarding this matter, remember always that what lives inside the receptor station that is the human being is vast. We live like the metaphorical iceberg, aware on a day-to-day basis of only a tiny portion of what we are actually connected to. Imprints from ancestors, residue from other life times, influences from what Carl Jung termed the collective unconscious, and who knows what else all lurk within cavernous layers beneath the surface.

The amazing thing is these collections of stuff literally move. They do not lie still. All the myriad of information, feeling, and experience continually shift around, and glimpses of what lies within our own vast "archives" touch from time to time upon our very small slice-of-the-pie perception.

For example: Ever had something happen in a dream that seemed so very different, so very foreign to your usual everyday kind of reality, but seemed so perfectly normal in the dream? So real? This is another manifestation of this phenomenon. Waking and dreaming are very much the same this way. Something filed away within you, perhaps even coming from the greater human collective, has stumbled into the light of your awareness.

So for the most part, it is arrogant to believe that we can even know why something has entered our experience or where it comes from, and for practical purposes, it simply doesn't matter. It is happening. The critical piece and what is important to always remember is that each time something comes to life for us it represents an opportunity to heal something, without exception. Each challenge literally becomes a place of honor as we take our rightful role as emissaries of light - for ourselves, our lineage, and the planet. Embracing this possibility means erasing all blame, including our own, and incorporating a tremendous level of personal power. Nobody need be blamed for anything.

So to conclude finally with our client example, the particular woman mentioned was exceptional in that she was very brave, and willing to be very honest. And this, combined with this wonderful way of viewing the spread, allowed us to do very deep work in a short amount of time.

Seeing this energy as clearly her own, a very natural, very healing conversation ensued. Together she and I talked through each one of her fears and came up with powerful new ways of thinking about her situation. We developed affirmations for her continuing work at home, to create and reinforce new pathways in the brain. We talked about specifics, like commitment for her needed to include freedom and permission to be completely herself, even her more "flaky" self. In some very pivotal moments, she agreed to give herself permission to change her mind at any time, even after committing, if she needed or wanted to. That she could make decisions based on her own well being, and that not "pleasing" someone did not equate to hurting someone, and on and on. And I had the clear sense as she walked away that she was taking the very first steps into a new life, at last breaking the spell of a long cycle. Priceless.

So now, tying this to the original concept set forth in this chapter, it is important to notice how once this client was able to embrace her situation and accept certain things about herself, everything shifted quite easily. She was free to keep her previous choices or make new ones.

*This way of working with the cards goes along very well with the practice of Ho'oponopono. This is an ancient Hawaiian shamanic practice streamlined and updated for modern day use that is based on this perspective of accepting energetic responsibility. I have used it on myself to great extent, and in fact can say there is not a day goes by when I do not use it.

For more information on Ho'oponopono and how to use it, I recommend the book by Joe Vitale called "Zero Limits: The Secret Hawaiian System for Wealth, Health, Peace, and More."

"THE SEVERED HEAD"

THIS IMAGE, APPEARING WITHIN THE DIAMOND SUIT, DEMONSTRATES THE INTENSE FOCUS POSSIBLE WITHIN CARDS OF THIS SUIT ASSOCIATED WITH THE ELEMENT OF FIRE. FIRE NOT ONLY WARMS, IT CAN BURN, AND SOMETIMES DESTROY EVEN THE THINGS WE MOST DESIRE. THIS LADY CLINGS, ENAMORED MOST BY WHAT SHE CANNOT HAVE.

YOU CAN FIND A WONDERFUL ORIGINAL STORY FOR THIS IMAGE IN "THE PLAYING CARD ORACLES" BOOK, A CLASSIC STYLE TALE DETAILING THE DANGERS OF THIS DYNAMIC ELEMENT AS IT MANIFESTS WITHIN THE INDIVIDUAL.

The Doors

THE ILLUSTRATION ABOVE SHOWS TWO VERY DIFFERENT, in fact *opposite* cards from a card reading perspective, yet how can this be? Both are nines, and both are in red suits - identical from a number and color point of view. So what is going on?

I want to take this opportunity to talk about a truly fantastic alchemical secret encoded into these decks of my father's, that up until now only the original "Charlie's Angels" have known of. That means only Lainey, Laddy, and myself - the 3 card muses of dearly departed "Charlie" - ever had this information. And being that everyone has evaporated now except me, I figure I better get this in writing somewhere.

This "secret" is really so juicy it didn't seem to have the proper space for inclusion in the already very full *Playing Card Oracles*. I always figured there would be a follow up book some day. So this is it. Truth is, I have only come to grasp the depth and breadth of it as time has passed. It was probably premature to write of it sooner.

The secret is in the nines, and it's known as "The Red Door" and "The Black Door," but to really understand "The Doors," we need a little primer in color and number from a playing card point of view. If you are already working with playing cards in divination, this will undoubtedly expand your perspectives. If not, it will give you insight all the same. The symbolism in playing cards is a profound language of alchemy.

Now it seems fairly straight forward that red and black symbolize opposites in many ways. They are the yin and yang of the deck - equally represented and equally powerful but in very different realms. But "The Doors" open another mystery: *opposites within the same color*. The two red suits demonstrate similar and sometimes dissimilar "red" tendencies, and same with the black. This is why two suits of each color are required in the deck, otherwise there would just be 26 cards all of one red suit and 26 cards of one black suit - or the suits would be green, red, yellow and blue.

So, the basic characteristics of the red and black colors and how they manifest in a reading are already outlined in *The Playing Card Oracles*, and so I will not be repetitive here. You can get the ebook for cheap. But the idea to get is that similarities as well as differences exist within the same color tendencies. Red, for example, speaks passion, but passion can include things like love and caring as well as jealousy, vindictiveness, and so forth. So you can see where we're going here.

And along with this magical aspect of opposites within one and the same color is the very powerful, very mystical potential represented by the number nine. Color and number together make the door.

So, of course there is a bit of a straightforward numerological definition for the nine, but to understand the door properly, let's see if we can't penetrate further into the mystery of this fascinating number. The thing to know is nine is the last number. It is an exit - just as the number one is an entrance. Why? Nine is the last number because nothing exists beyond it. Period. There is nothing except remixes and rehash of what has already come before. The ten for example, the number following nine, is a combination of one and zero. We are starting over. So we must think of the numbers as a pathway of chronology if we are to unlock their secrets.

So there are two choices here. Do you understand? IF I have mastered the lessons of each and every number up to and including the nine, I can use the vibration of the nine to literally exit this world and the human experience and pass through the doors. If I haven't, I get to relive, rerun, and re-experience what *I have already experienced* through reincarnation, repeating life patterns, etc... - basically new combinations of what has already come before. So once I actually get what I came into the physical experience to get, the nine is my fire escape. It is the final final.

So, the cool thing about these doors within the playing cards is they reveal *how* to exit. And we use this mystic portal for little and big escapes. Anytime we "graduate" from certain life experiences, or complete our circle of learning within any one arena we get a little exit. And then of course, there is "the big exit," when you have mastered the whole of human experience and you get to chassé out of this world altogether.

But remember, to use the door is exceptional. The most common experience of the nine is to use it as a *temporary ending*, followed by the usual previous lessons showing up in new ways. I am on the hamster wheel, and I get to try again.

So how do I know what kind of ending I am looking at when nines appear? You know a final escape because one of the doors shows up. It is exceptional to have both nines of the same color appear in a reading.

The Red Door:

9♡ "uncontrolled" ---------- 1 ---------- "disciplined" 9◇

The Black Door:

9♤ "corrupt" ---------- 1 ---------- "pure" 9♧

So when two nines of the same color appear next to each other, the question to ask is, "How do these two cards reconcile each other?" Or specifically, how do victim and perpetrator exist side by side? or angel and devil? or right and wrong? or disciplined and uncontrolled? How do they find peace with each other? This is the question, and the answer opens the door. It is integrating *the whole* of the red or black experience, end to end.

The other feature of the number nine that makes the doorway work is that because nine is at the end of the path of numbers, it encompasses the experience of all the other numbers that came before, and because it is the biggest single number (remember no numbers exist after nine,) then it is the number of extremes. So you get the maximum experience in both directions - good and bad. No other number gives you the gamut. This is why people who align with cards of the number nine are people who have a tough time with moderation. Like that old saying, *"...and when she was good, she was very, very good, and when she was bad she was horrid!"*

And of course, we want to be "good" and "pure" and "disciplined." We want to "lean toward the right" of the above diagram. But the doorway is showing us something else. It is saying that within us lies the *spectrum*. The doorway *must* have two panels. It is a double door. And the entrance is *between* all concepts of good and bad. The still point in the center of the diagram is where the door opens. It is the eye of the needle. We see *all* that we have within us, all the contradictions, and we *identify with nothing. Concepts are replaced by awareness.* And we choose awareness - impartial - and in it find something which transcends the pendulum swing.

It is fascinating when you read the previous chapter "Puppet Strings," with this doorway in mind. There was a golden moment in the example reading where the client had the realization of two opposing sides of herself simultaneously. She saw her repeating destruction of relationships coexisting alongside her diligent efforts to manifest monogamy and commitment. *But they had to come together in her consciousness for her to pass through the doorway of transformation.*

Amazingly, this doorway actually appeared in her reading. The 9 of Diamonds was laid on the table, and the 9 of Hearts directly below it, touching it. In fact, the 9 of Hearts was upside down - literally *mirroring* the nine above it. Unbelievable. I maybe wouldn't trust my own memory of this except in good fortune I happened to take a photograph of the layout while it was still on the table. So this demonstrates how this client was really on the verge of merging these two parts of herself, and the reading was the push that she needed, with perfect timing. Truly she is finished with this lesson.

And so what is beyond the nine, through the door? It is another metaphysical precept I am going to throw at you, and it is called "the Upper Kingdom." It is an alternative name for "the court," but only comes into play when one has crossed the red or black threshold. Otherwise, the courts are courts. They are personalities - complex, yes, but bound to cycles of repetition and suffering through identification. But courts as they exist as part of the Upper Kingdom, are GODS. Do you see? We are talking about two planes of existence, one alongside the other - ghost reflections of each other - but having different levels of vibration and power. One is transcendent, and one more dense and less powerful - one in control of destiny, the other at the mercy of destiny.

By the way, in the playing card decks illustrated by my father, ten's are always court cards. They are not lower numbered cards as traditionally depicted. Everything after nine is a court. This has historical precedent, and also fits entirely perfectly from a numerological point of view. Again, all is discussed in *The Playing Card Oracles* so no need to over aspirate myself here. Get *The Playing Card Oracles,* if you haven't already.

So, it's not like the idea of an alchemical doorway doesn't exist anywhere else, but it is obscure, even from a metaphysical point of view. But my dad was good at obscure. He was a scholar of weird. But the part that is truly mind boggling is that he *saw* these arcane secrets of alchemy in the regular 52 card playing deck. ...Huh? And this was in the 1970's, mind you. And he saw them *in detail*. Now, being an offshoot of my father, it has occurred to my near equally strange mind that the explanation for this is quite possibly very simple. What if my father was the person (or part of a group of persons) who actually *encoded* these secrets into the original 52 card deck centuries ago at it's inception, and simply re-appeared at the ordained time to reveal them? Color me nut cakes, but why not?

Isn't it possible that the playing card deck is a time capsule, a book of alchemical secrets hidden in plain site? And if you were the one who created this time capsule, wouldn't you want it decoded like *right now*, as our entire world stands at the very precipice of utter God-knows-what? And wouldn't the visionaries who encoded this knowledge be not only the ones with the vested interest, but also the explicit ability to see their mission through to completion?

Or was it pure happenstance that my father came along precisely when he did and saw what he did? To me this is the explanation that is farfetched.

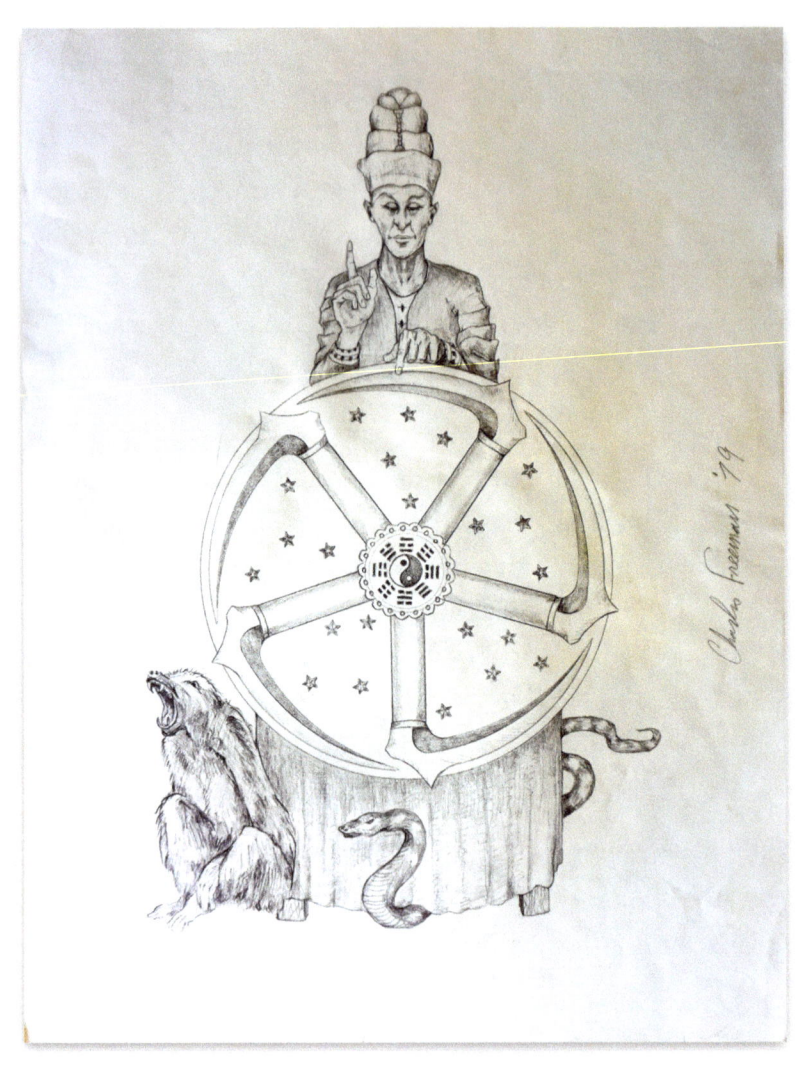

FROM AN EARLY NOTEBOOK

The Acid Test: Ridiculous Happiness

WITH ALL THIS TALK OF TRANSCENDENCE and personal evolution, let us ground ourselves in something ultimately practical, ultimately measurable. Really, there is only one exhilarating outcome that is the reason for embarking on any of this: I am happy. And this is the measure of my success as a card reader. If I do not feel ridiculously happy after employing all these wonderful techniques, something somewhere has gone astray.

Why? Because if I am truly of service to the person I am reading for, truly facilitating higher level energies to enter that person's world for transformation and healing, I am giving. And if I am giving, I must, by cosmic decree, be receiving.

The truth is, it is impossible to truly give something without instantly receiving what has been given. This is the cosmic law that John Lennon coined so well in the song, "Instant Karma."

Karma and the law of giving and receiving is something that, when viewed from a purely physical perspective, takes time. If I rip someone off, it's just a matter of time, for example, 'til I get ripped off in some way. But from an energetic perspective, the exchange happens right damn now. Always the energetic first, then the physical (being slower vibrating) catches up later.

So if I am sensitive and honest with myself, I can see and measure *within myself* exactly what I have given the client. The question to ask immediately following a reading is, "How do I *feel?*"

So I can read all the five star books on card reading, take all the classes, have the very latest, coolest deck with all the nice pictures, but if I feel like crap after I give a reading, guess what I have facilitated? So I need to go back and evaluate.

After a great reading, there is a deep sense of satisfaction and peace. I wear a smile on the inside, and I feel as though I am making a difference in the world - that what I do is truly important. And it doesn't matter how tough the cards or the dynamics represented. Healing is intrinsically hard work sometimes, but this is different then bringing someone down. A tear now and then in the reading is normal. But healing is liberating, satisfying.

And right alongside all of this liberation and happiness, I must fully recognize I have zero control over what the client's reaction is. I give every reading with love, integrity, honesty, and transformative potential, and still the client can walk away let down, depressed, angry, or whatever. And so it is.

I have been surprised to find just how many people are really in search of something simply to pacify themselves. But never ever am I to become a simple vendor of flowers dipped in sugar. I have to "grow up" in a way, and let go of my need to please people, while fully committing to satisfying myself.

And here is the final bonus feature of the "happiness test."

What if, just what if, each and every one of the readings that I do for someone else is really my own? And I mean exactly this. What if everything that enters into my experience as a reader is an opportunity for healing for me myself, and the client just happens to be there delivering the steaming goods like the pizza delivery guy?

Because what I give and what I get in a reading are one and the same, every encounter with a client is as important for me as it is for the person sitting across from me. How can it be otherwise? And in the great glory of the intelligent universe, I observe how every session I do "for someone else" embodies some aspect of my own psyche that it is time for me to look at. So a reading is self serving in the very best sense. I get to address and resolve stuff about myself that I never even suspect, clearing out karma before it has the chance to manifest in my life. I am sweeping and sweeping and cleaning and cleaning interior worlds, literally bypassing years of traditional counseling or even life times of good old trial and error - for the client, yes hopefully - but for myself, without fail.

"FORTUNA," LADY OF DIAMONDS

ME - SKIPPING, HOPPING, FROLICKING, AND OTHERWISE TWIRLING INTO FURNITURE AND OTHER SOLID OBJECTS AFTER GIVING A GOOD READING.

Spider Vision

SOMETHING ELSE WORTH REMARKING ON occurs when you successfully employ evolutionary techniques in your readings: evolutionary life changes.

This is yet another "acid test." Along with the "ridiculous happiness" mentioned in the previous chapter, what follows is another indication that something has gone really right in your readings. And I have witnessed it from years of follow up with my clients, but it's not the kind of follow up you would expect for a reading.

Traditional follow ups for a session tend to consist of some kind of report as to whether the reading "came true" or not. What we will talk about in this chapter is really just the opposite. "Coming true" cannot be the measure of a reading whose goal is transformation. We need new measures if our beloved art is to survive the planetary evolution that is already occurring.

The truth is, glimpses into other time periods are typically afforded precisely because we are being given the opportunity to alter something, to embrace a different choice. So shedding light on something changes the very thing that is being observed.

This is simple science, and as readers of the future we must incorporate science. Laboratory processes demonstrate that chemical reactions which ordinarily take place in the dark, for example, change completely when taking place under the laboratory light. And this is exactly what happens as we shed the light of our attention on things which formerly belonged to the dark of the unconscious. Nothing is or ever can be as it was before the reading. So good readings have a way of sabotaging themselves as far as the old standby measure of "coming true." Coming true just means nothing has changed.

A better measure than "coming true," for starters, would be "ringing true." As readers, we become sensitive to what it feels like to "strike a chord." There is an energy conveyed when hitting on something, like the sound of a guitar string perfectly in tune. This resonation is shifting energy, shifting reality. And follow up with the clients works in tandem with this objective.

So when I do follow up now, I ask weird questions, because I am looking for something the client may not be associating with the fact they just received a reading. I ask if anything "unusual" happened shortly following. I am looking for symptoms of shift: things like an unexpected phone call from someone they have not talked to in years, for example; or they arrive home to find the room mate has re-arranged the living room furniture; or someone in their life makes some sort of comment or personal announcement that is super "out of character." Often, things that seem small are the very things that indicate big shifts. They herald changes in what I call time lines. But let me explain.

The way I have observed it, a person's life is much like a spider web. We travel along a particular silky thread and this is our daily life. At certain points in the web, threads intersect, allowing certain "cross roads." It is at these particular points where we have the opportunity to change course, and travel a different but related thread within the web that is our life. But only at these crossing points.

Much of the time, in fact the majority of time, we do not "cross over," either because we do not see the opportunity, or we do not choose it. To stay on the same course or "time line" means I am keeping my previous perspectives and my previous choices.

When a person comes for a reading, typically they are tired of traveling a particular thread, but they don't know how to change trajectory. Readings coincide with these points or moments of glimmering possibility within the web. This is in fact why the reading is occurring when it is. So my job, in essence, is to facilitate this shift. And always, when these life changes actually occur, there are signals to that effect. We just have to be alert to them.

There are all kinds of movies out now that illustrate just the same idea, and they are so much more fun to watch when you have this "insider" information about time lines. Some of the ones that come to mind are "Run Lola Run," "Source Code," "Donnie Darko," and "The Family Man." I seek out films that have these kind of themes, and have been delighted to see just how many there are now. The idea is entering mass consciousness in a big way, and I believe this influx is nothing less than a "preview" of what is to become common understanding as we enter a truly cosmic era on planet Earth.

So start thinking "time lines" in your own life, and pay attention to things that seem surprising, out of the ordinary, or out of sequence. Did you just jump into a new time line, a new life trajectory? Notice what else happened right before that may have facilitated a shift. Embrace your "inner spider."

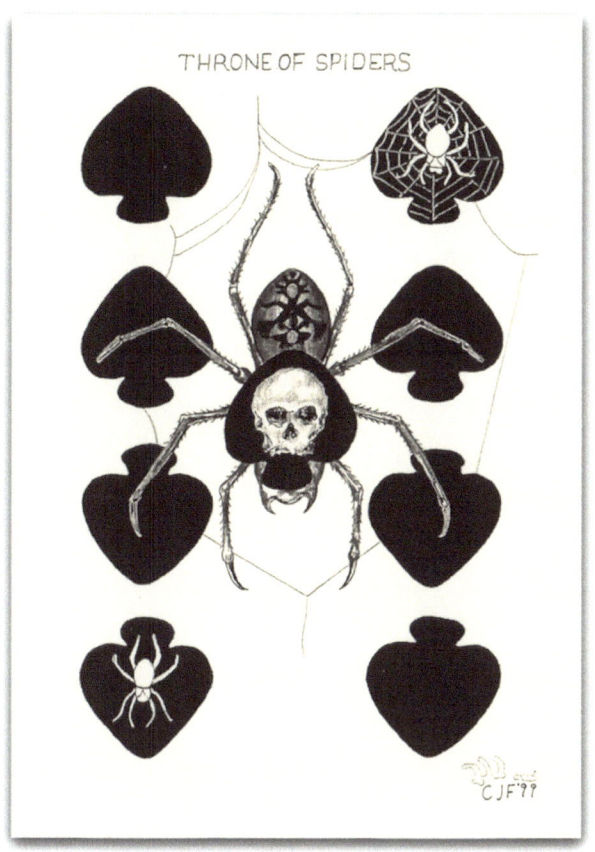

9 OF SPADES, THE "THRONE OF SPIDERS."

NINES ARE DIFFICULT CARDS - ALWAYS. THEY ARE CARDS OF CHALLENGE, LIKE ALL ODD NUMBERED CARDS. WITH THIS NINE IN PARTICULAR, IT IS COMMON TO SEE HEAVY SITUATIONS AND THE BURDENS ASSOCIATED WITH THIS PINNACLE NUMBER MANIFESTING THROUGH THE DENSELY VIBRATING SUIT OF EARTH. THE THING I LIKE ABOUT HAVING THIS CARD HERE IN THE TEXT IS IT DEMONSTRATES ANOTHER POSSIBILITY: AS WE BECOME MORE AWARE AS HUMAN BEINGS, WE BECOME MORE AWARE OF THE WORKINGS BEHIND PHYSICAL REALITY. THE SPIDER IS THE SPINNER, WEAVING THE LUMINOUS THREADS THAT CONNECT ALL THINGS TOGETHER. SO THE QUESTION WHEN ENCOUNTERING THIS CARD IS, ARE YOU GOING TO BE BIT BY THIS OLD SPINSTER OR WILL YOU ENTER INTO HER SECRETS?

Weapons and Playthings

CARDS IN THEMSELVES ARE NEUTRAL, but once I begin channeling energy and intention through them, they do not remain so. They become real tools, and will either help or harm - nothing in between. In this deceptively humble profession of "card reader," I must become ultimately skilled - like a surgeon armed with electricity and knives.

And as I practice and embody the techniques offered in this book, this becomes more and more the case. I am not having a casual conversation with someone as I read for them. It just cannot be. I vibrate. I am an energy worker. And no matter what the cards, what the words I choose, my presence does and will effect the person I am sitting with.

And people will remember the reading for a long time. I am "the oracle," "the seer," the one who doles out destinies - even if in their conscious mind, they are telling themselves it is all "silly." People will remember cards, and words that I say, but they will remember them as their imagination re-writes the story over time - not as it occurred. It is surprising to me how very infrequently does a client's recollection of a reading actually match my own.

So what are we dealing with here? I will become what the client wants me to be, and the reading the same. And whatever the client's wish or intention for their own life, I will fit within that. Not I nor anyone else cannot change this. It is spiritual law. It is why I cannot help everyone, and it is why I cannot save everyone - at least from a traditional point of view.

So what is the point if a person's own will is the determining factor anyway? If someone's wish is to truly improve their experience here on Earth, yes, I can assist with that. But no matter what the situation, I can bring awareness to someone. Always I arrive with an opportunity for self knowledge in my little bag of 52. And in the end, my own feeling is this is the most valuable thing. The client receives an opportunity to become more self empowered, to gain something for their own arsenal in learning their own lessons, but it may not entail the path I or they envision. Gifts come wrapped strangely.

So learning and progressing within my profession I myself traverse the epic landscapes of symbolism offered by my cards. I build a rich language beyond words for my own path of self knowledge. I ally with, confront, and question suits, numbers, and concepts, and watch as my perceptions of one and the same cards shift - as if being viewed through the haze of a dream. And now as I approach the esteemed "hag" status, I find myself aligning more and more with cards of the number nine. Aha! The doorway!

And the clients that I do see now for readings fall into more distinct categories of extremes. I am miracle worker, life saver. I am destroyer. I am your ultimate nightmare. So watch out! People have been broken by the misinterpretation of my words because their fears became triggered, and people who wish to hear only compliments speak behind my back and try to destroy me. So the territory does *not* become easier - it becomes more dangerous. The risks get bigger, and the payoffs, accordingly. And I am a warrior. I am here to heal and I accept the challenges. I proceed.

And, I learn. I become more and more skillful, examining myself and how I can become better, more precise, and more scientific with the use of my tools to get the results I want more and more often. And there is no school that teaches card reading on this level. So I teach and learn myself, and I take the risks.

And the readings that do not go as I would like offer my greatest learning opportunities. They are my greatest gift as a being seeking self realization. So always I am taking responsibility. As a transformational reader I MUST be able to take criticism. I must be able to truly look at *myself*, as I ask the client to do, and see where *my* weaknesses are. Do I want to be better, or am I like the client that only wishes to hear compliments?

So I am being tough here because I want you to seriously ask yourself if this way of reading is for you or not. It is my last ditch attempt to save you from unnecessary personal anguish. There is no way the techniques in this book can be undertaken without invoking powerful forces. It cannot be a casual foray. So if you do not have the wish or personal fortitude to see through what will be set into motion, think of this as a book of fairytales. Put it back on the shelf for some other day. And yet I tell you, I know of no better practice than that of transformational card reading to get to truly know yourself. So consider carefully your next move.

And a final word in this final chapter on cards as weapons. Remember always, a blade has two edges - and depending how it is used we get the benefit or the damage. There is perhaps no better demonstration of this in cards than in the practice of reading for oneself. One can see undeniably what the results of your actions are when the blade is turned on yourself.

Here I cannot help but think of Luke from Star Wars, stuck in the swamp with Yoda, first learning how to use "the force" and the light saber. Ha! There are so many mistakes to be made! And this we should expect within our own craft of power. To become a true master, we need to know all the pitfalls. But conversely, there is no need to tarry in what does not serve.

The use of cards for oneself is a slippery slope in the swamp of card reading training ground. Many have perished here, and left pieces of their soul littered among the ground. This is a pursuit that requires such delicacy, such finesse, it is normal to experience a learning curve. But learn quickly! It is a wonderful gift to be able to use cards well for oneself, and a wretched curse to be trapped by it.

Detachment is key. And yet detachment is a tall order when you have become emotionally involved in something, and of course, this is the precise time when you want advice from the cards. So be crystal clear. Advice is not the same as pacification. And the difference is everything.

My own big lesson in this regard came many years ago while going through a real gut wrenching divorce. I seriously abused myself with cards by seeking comfort from them that was not there. As mentioned in Part One, I used to sit in closets during this period. Well there were times I would sit in there and shuffle - shuffle, shuffle, shuffle. And ask, and ask, and ask. And I watched how the cards morphed. It was a game of mirrors and it injured me energetically. I could feel this damn hole right where my solar plexus is - about the size of a baseball - and it took a long time before I couldn't feel it anymore. And that sucks.

Since then, I keep cards at arms length when it comes to issues that most engage me. I do not *depend* on them. I check in, as it is a continuing part of my own study, but I walk away. I find other, more creative ways of working with cards that fortify me rather than drain me. My one cardinal rule is never *ever* do I ask the same question twice.

Repeating questions is the "original sin," so to speak, in this work with cards for oneself. It begins a game, and opens a sort of bloodletting on an energetic level. Remember always, cards can never be benign. You are conjuring, and you beckon energies. Of course we all know there is "good" as well as "bad" out there, in other words, entities that do or do not have your best interest in mind, and if you choose to be guided by insecurities, desperation, or the like, then the path that ensues will be accordingly dark.

The only qualifying admonitions I will give here are 1) If I really don't "get" the message given from the original question, I allow myself one clarifying card, and 2) Re-wording a question that has already been asked is the same as repeating a question, and is part of the slippery slyness of this game. So this goes back to the importance of making sure the original question is formulated the way you want it in the first place.

And of course, it is natural and expected for clients in distress to try to take the reins and coerce you to repeat questions for them. So it is up to you to make sure *you* are the one in charge of your own readings, not the client. Sticking with what you have already received, whether it be for yourself or someone else, is the best way to maintain integrity and make your readings work for you, and not against you. Swallow the bitter pill.

Now, in hindsight, I can see how consulting cards for myself with restraint has forced a kind of maturity for me. I had to "get over myself" in a way, and came to understand how cards are a kind of puzzle language that provide stepping stones rather than solid answers. I learned that strength and also happiness come from a process of trust within what is yet unknown.

And isn't it funny where the path will lead? The moments I feel most sure lead me further into moments where I am completely unsure - like the clever breadcrumbs that led Hansel and Gretel yet deeper into the woods. Answers lead to questions. And I take these steps into the darkness, knowing it will literally forge who I am.

But cards are not only weapons, not only something to "fear and revere." They are toys. But this in no way decreases their value. In fact, it increases it. We have to turn our perspectives about "toys" and "play" around as adults, especially as adult readers of cards.

When viewed from the "mature" adult perspective, cards are simple, silly toys, like a doll or a plastic tug boat that we put away in the cupboard when play time is over. They are a game, this is true. And through cards, we can be children again. But always remember, for the adult to invite their own inner child is an act of great power.

Children are brilliant learners, and very much outweigh adults in terms of their ability to learn. They are the olympic athletes of learning. And what do children love more than anything else? They love to play. And we as adults are so good at being so serious, priding ourselves in how much we work and how we have "no time" for play. Maybe this is precisely why our brains are turning into crust.

And much as children act out or mimic different play scenarios or stories, cards too offer this. Good cards have the ability to mimic or model life. They animate a microcosmic world, with the scope and flexibility to portray any possible scenario. With good cards in hand, the sky is the limit.

So, if you are having trouble imagining with your cards, first ask yourself if you have a proper deck and system. If so, it may not be your cards. It may just be your rusty adult imagination. But no need to fret. The prescription is simple: more play. We all once knew how to play. We can play again.

Allow the cards to lure you out of your adult mind and into your imagination. Let the cards twist and meld, like a magic mirror. Give yourself permission to have a daydream of sorts. But different than an ordinary daydream, this dream will be given life by the cards. You can see it on the table in front of you. You can shuffle it, rearrange it, and make believe outcomes and possibilities that are new to you. Breakthroughs are common in readings, unlike ordinary daydreams which tend to simply reinforce previous perspectives.

And my plaything has become a power tool, once again.

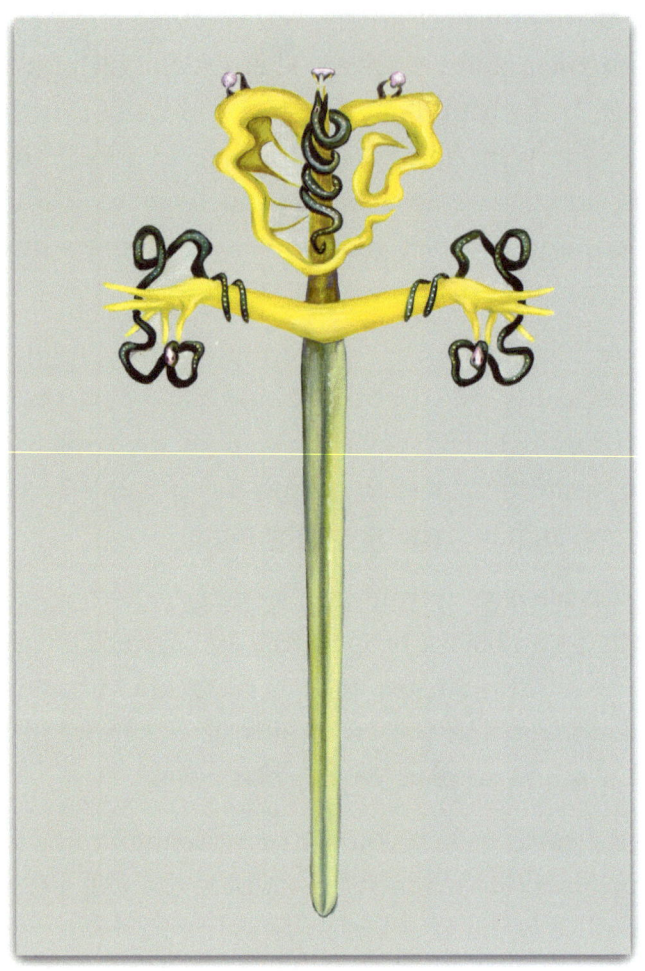

THE SWORD

THE SEVEN IS THE POWER TOOL IN THE DECK, AND WOULD BE MORE PROPERLY ILLUSTRATED IF MY DAD HAD PAINTED A BIG MOTOR ON IT! SIMILAR TO A NINE, CARDS OF THE NUMBER SEVEN REPRESENT "FLIP SIDE" POSSIBILITIES, SINCE EACH BLADE MUST BY DEFINITION HAVE TWO SIDES, AND SOMETIMES THE EDGE BETWEEN THE TWO IS VERY FINE, INDEED.

THIS PAINTING SERVED AS THE IMAGE FOR ALL CARDS OF THE NUMBER SEVEN IN THIS SERIES. ONLY THE SUIT SIGNS CHANGED, AND WITH IT THE REALM IN WHICH THE SWORD FUNCTIONS. SEVEN IS INDEED A MAGIC NUMBER, PROVIDING A CRITICAL AND EXCITING IMPLEMENT FOR INNER WORK.

In Closing

So, in the end, card reading has the potential to be so very much more than "card reading." Perhaps someone someday will come up with a better title for this occupation. I have tried, but ultimately everything feels contrived. My recent line of thinking is that perhaps "card reader" is actually a good title, for it is so lack luster there is no opportunity for the ego to thrive upon it. After all, humility is a vital quality, most especially for those striving for the ultimate prize: the transmutation of scrap metal into gold, as in the original definition for alchemy given in the introduction to this book.

To me, there is a freedom in cards. They are not something precious from a traditional point of view. They are precious like a flower is precious. They are fleeting, born to crumble in the wind. Their true value always only will be their ability to point me back to myself. The glyphs and pictures symbolize what is *inside of me*, and through their use I learn to manage these very powerful, otherwise hidden forces.

And so, as humble "card readers," let our mastery remain within the invisible realms - our treasure, sublime. We will be true magicians! Let us focus not on distractions, on feats of psychic ability nor predictions of future events, for as a focus, these are ego driven. Let us be of the greatest service possible, and let this be determined by the all seeing intelligence of beneficent Spirit, beyond the mortal scope.

Let us never forget, the more powerful one becomes, the more delicious one is to the ego. As mentioned before, the risks and temptations do not lessen progressing in this work. They increase. So let us be steadfast, forever aware of where true glory is found.

And finally, and perhaps most ironically, let our work be for the small things, for the small is what is under our feet at this moment. It is the one place where transformation can actually take place. So let what we do be ultimately practical, helping us to be better in each here and now - better mothers, fathers, sisters and brothers. For what beauty is in the starry sky if we lay tossing and turning beneath it? So let us lift from the lowest level.

And from this place of firm footing upon the small, let our practice lead us into greater communion with something very expansive within ourselves, that we may find the true meaning of joy here on Earth.

Amen

SERVANT OF THE MEEK

TERRENE, SERVANT OF THINGS SMALL. ULTIMATELY ANCHORED TO THE HERE AND NOW MOMENT THROUGH HER SUIT OF EARTH (SPADES) - AND MEEK, AS SYMBOLIZED BY HER POSITION ON THE GROUND. THIS GODDESS IS NOT OF HIGH RANKING LIKE THE QUEEN OF HER SUIT, AND YET THIS AFFORDS HER THE HUMILITY THAT GIVES THIS CARD ITS' POWER. IT IS A BEAUTIFUL REFERENCE POINT FOR US ALL.

About the Author/Illustrator

Ana Cortez is a hard to pin down woman, who frequently defines herself by the many rotating card personalities found in playing cards. Her previous titles include *The Playing Card Oracles, A Source Book for Divination*, and *The Teacher Within, Enraptured Ranting and Other Tales*.

She lives with her husband in a small adobe surrounded by thorns and guarded by fierce rescue dogs in Santa Fe, NM. Her website is http://www.anacortez.com

C.J. Freeman was a writer and self taught artist who illustrated playing decks for divination and wrote several volumes (due for publishing) centered around the subject of card reading with playing cards. He exited this world in 2010.

www.ingramcontent.com/pod-product-compliance
Lightning Source LLC
Chambersburg PA
CBHW042307230426
43662CB00031B/62